# Buddy Reading

# Buddy Reading

## CROSS-AGE TUTORING IN A MULTICULTURAL SCHOOL

### Katharine Davies Samway
### Gail Whang
### Mary Pippitt

HEINEMANN
PORTSMOUTH, NH

**Heinemann**
A division of Reed Elsevier Inc.
361 Hanover Street
Portsmouth, NH 03801–3912

*Offices and agents throughout the world*

**Library of Congress Cataloging-in-Publication Data**
Samway, Katharine Davies.
    Buddy reading : cross-age tutoring in a multicultural
school / Katharine Davies Samway, Gail Whang & Mary
Pippitt.
        p.    cm.
    Includes bibliographical references (p.        ).
    ISBN 0–435–08840–8
    1. Peer-group tutoring of students—California—Case studies.
2. Reading (Elementary)—California—Case studies.   3. Literacy
programs—California—Case studies.   4. Education, Bilingual—
California—Case studies.   5. Interpersonal relations—California—
Case studies.   I. Whang, Gail.   II. Pippitt, Mary.
III. Title.
LB1031.5.S36   1995
37.3′94—dc20
                                                    94–41378
                                                    CIP

Acquisitions Editor: Leigh Peake
Production Editor: Renée M. Pinard
Cover Designer: Darci Mehall

Printed in the United States of America on acid-free paper.
    02 03    VP        6 7

We dedicate this book to the students whose
thoughts, words, and actions are discussed in the
pages that follow. We have grown tremendously
from what they have taught us.

# Contents

# Acknowledgments

Many people have helped us write this book. In particular, we are most grateful to the students with whom we have worked over the past six years as we have implemented buddy reading. Jenny Rienzo was a wonderful research assistant, helping us to see things in different ways. Raiida Thompson did an excellent job of transcribing audiotapes and providing us with feedback. We have shared drafts of the book with many friends and their comments have been invaluable to us—thank you Tom Samway, Kathy Booker, Mike Bowen, Sonja Ebel, Norm Gusner, Michael Hagan, Sonny Kim, Charlotte Knox, Madeleine Lee, Gloria Norton, Stephanie Steffey, and Carlyn Syvanen. Arlene Graham has been a principal whose vision and leadership allowed us to continue the buddy reading odyssey.

We are appreciative of our many Instructional Assistants, Nitayane Youmagul, Somsy Phonexaysitthidet, Consuelo David, Graciela Delgadillo, Hilda Menjivar, and Rosie Rodriguez for all the special help they have given to the children.

This book has taken many months to write and our families have been more than supportive. Thank you to Tom, Patrick, Brian-Martin and Tomás Samway for your constant support and understanding. Thank you to Daniel and Karl Gusner who filled me in on the exciting highlights of the many ballgames I had to miss, Chris Dobie who encouraged and chauffered them to their games, and to Norm Gusner who never failed to have a delicious gourmet dinner waiting after long evenings of writing. Thank you to Omar Hernandez for his hospitality and continual understanding.

# 1

## "When Are We Doing Buddy Reading?"

## Buddy Reading in Action

It's Tuesday morning recess and it's raining outside. In fact, it's pouring, so the fifth- and sixth-grade students in Gail Whang's class stay inside, working on one of the computers, playing board games on the floor, or chatting at the oblong tables that fill the room. The rain is unusual in Oakland at this time of year, but what really catches our attention today is sixth grader Amphaivane. She is sitting alone at a table reading a picture book. The worn wooden chair cradles her as she props the book on the scratched desktop. We can see that she is softly reading aloud, as if to another person. Her lips move, and we can hear the cadence in her voice as she alternates characters. We can see the subtle expression that she is putting into the reading and how momentarily she becomes the characters in the book. We stop our conversation to watch. We realize that she is practicing for the buddy reading session that will follow recess.

After recess, when the rain has temporarily subsided, fifteen first and second graders from Mary Pippitt's class change places with fifteen fifth and sixth graders from Gail's class. This is a weekly routine that the students are familiar with and look forward to. A haphazard line of younger children is waiting patiently outside the door to the upper grade classroom located across the concrete patio (see Photo 1). They are carrying picture books and notebooks under their arms, which they glance at from time to time. They push against each other in an attempt to locate their buddies inside the classroom. Animated faces peer through the small wedge of glass. Those who have the clearest view wave to Richard, who is sitting next to the door and closest to the window. He smiles, waves back, and returns

PHOTO 1    *First and second graders wait outside the upper grade classroom.*

his attention to Gail, who is finishing a minilesson on how to read non-fiction picture books to young readers. It's hard for Richard to concentrate, though, as he can see his buddy, Sammy, who is mouthing a greeting to him and waving excitedly.

After a couple of minutes, Richard leans over and opens the door. A human exchange takes place. As Sammy and his peers enter the classroom, fifteen fifth/sixth graders leave to work with their buddies in the primary classroom across the way. The two classes merge. Students greet each other and inquire about the books their partners have selected. Twelve-year-old Ricardo calls out to his first-grade buddy, "Hey, Malcolm, hurry up," as he leafs through *The Very Hungry Caterpillar* (Carle 1981). Six students leave with Ms. Phoutaboum, the instructional assistant, who each week takes three pairs of students to cook during buddy reading. Within minutes, pairs of students are working together, reading favorite books, talking about them, selecting other books, and drawing and writing responses to the books (see Photo 2). Amphaivane, an eleven-year-old girl who is usually acutely shy, is reading aloud to seven-year-old Sung (see Photo 3). Her voice resonates with animation. From time to time, Richard and Sammy, who are sitting across from Amphaivane and her partner, stop their reading, glance up and listen for a few moments. "Let me read that when you're finished," calls out Richard.

PHOTO 2    *A buddy reading session.*

PHOTO 3    *A buddy reading pair.*

Across the room, eleven-year-old José is having a hard time getting and keeping six year-old Lim's attention. He nudges and admonishes him, "Pay attention. You have to pay attention." Twelve-year-old George, who is sitting at an adjacent table, suggests, "Try another book. He don't like it." Gail is watching this interaction from across the room, and when she senses that José needs guidance, she moves to his side and asks how things are going. She is constantly moving around the room, listening in, taking notes for future reference, and quietly praising and offering advice to students whenever appropriate.

There is a gentle hum in the two classrooms. Something of a transformation has occurred. Students like thirteen-year-old Antoine, who has difficulty interacting with others without conflict, is gentle and thoughtful with his much smaller buddy, Souksavath. Amphaivane, usually so reserved, is vivacious and a knowledgeable resource to her peers. Juan, a twelve year-old who is used to getting his own way, is nurturing—he pulls his partner close to him, wraps an arm around his shoulder and listens carefully to what he says. María, who is most comfortable speaking Spanish and does not usually speak up in class, is confident, resourceful, and animated. Richard, a struggling, frustrated reader who often erupts into angry outbursts, is patient with his lively partner, even though reading the picture books is an ordeal for him.

At the end of about thirty minutes, the students return to their respective classrooms, where they immediately reflect upon the buddy reading experience. In the first/second grade classroom, the discussion begins with Mary asking them how the session went:

MARY: How was buddy reading today? Especially as some of you had a new buddy.
LEE: Better.
SUNG: I like it because my buddy say I read good. She say it to me.
MARY: You got a compliment. [Sung nods in agreement.]
MANOP: Fun. My buddy draws good.
SOUNTHAVY: Boring. 'Cuz the story was too much long.
MARY: So, yours was too long? What will you do next time?
SOUNTHAVY: Pick a short one. [Pause.]
ENRIQUE: It was good 'cuz I read a whole book.

The discussion continues in this way, with the students commenting on their accomplishments, what their buddies did and said, positive aspects of the experience, and problems they encountered. The raising of problems is an integral part of the debriefing as it gives the students a chance to consciously contemplate the origins of the problems and ways in which they can improve the buddy reading session. This discussion is a means for the students to celebrate their accomplishments, and share with and learn from each other. It is also a mechanism for Mary to stay in touch with what is occurring in the two classrooms during buddy reading. As she listens to the children's comments, Mary realizes that before the next buddy reading session she needs to conduct a minilesson on how to pick an appropriate book.

In the fifth/sixth-grade classroom, the students first reflect in writing on their experiences. Gail asks them to think about how the session went and why it went the way it did. The students open their logs and write. The room is quiet. Only the scratches of pencils and pens on paper interrupt the silence. Like their younger buddies, the fifth and sixth graders share successes, raise questions, and ponder problems. For example, Soheila writes that she thinks the book that she and Yien Fou read was too long, as her buddy had been looking around a lot. In her reflections, Tamara comments on the strategies her buddy used and his preferred reading choices:

> Today Sangkhom was looking at me read. If I asked him to read he would. But not all the time. He told me what to write. And if he said a word wrong he would go back and sound it out. He did alot better today. My buddy Sangkhom also picked a book he could read. And he read most of the book. He didn't need much help. And I think that the book[s] I got for him he didn't like them very much. But 1 of the storys he liked I liked also. And we talked about what we thoug[ht] was going to haddend [happen]. He didn't do that. And we also talked about the parts we liked. I think he likes more short storys then big ones.

Aromrack, a student whose first language is Laotian, writes about how she is noticing changes in her buddy:

> What I noticed about my buddy was that she starting to read by herself to me. Usaully she let me read to her instead. She also starting to write by herself and usaully she let me write in her logs, but now she did it all by herself and she only let me read the book that was hard for her but she read 6 pages and I read the rest. Buddy reading was great because my buddy is paying more attention to me and she never talk that much when I ask her if she like the book but it was okay even though she doesn't talk that much. She told me that she like being with me and I was shocked, I was also happy too.

Not all the students had a successful buddy reading experience and they share their frustrations and concerns in their logs. George writes:

> Today Manop didn't get better but worser becuase he still doesn't listen to me, at least a little while ago he listened to me reading

and he still can't read or write. Problems: Does not read. Does
not listen.

After writing their reflections for about ten minutes, the class sits
on the rug for a whole class debriefing session. The class usually
begins the session by talking about what went well, and today is no
exception. Nam begins the discussion by commenting, "It's going
fine." He then goes on to explain that his partner wanted Nam to
read to him, which has never happened before. Nam feels that this
illustrates that his partner is starting to feel more comfortable with
him. Tamara comments that she is proud whenever her buddy reads
on his own, "without my helping him." She takes pleasure in seeing
how her efforts are paying off. After sharing their successes, Gail asks
the students to share any questions they have or problems they
encountered. Soheila begins. She says, "I'm having trouble getting a
discussion going. When I ask a question, my buddy answers, 'I don't
know.'" The rest of the class sits quietly for a few moments and then
students begin to ask for clarification and offer suggestions. Juan
asks, "What you read?" It was a book about animals and Viliphone
follows up with, "Does she like animals?" Soheila isn't sure. The students continue exploring the topic, and then Gail asks Soheila if she
shared her own responses to the book. Soheila shakes her head and
Gail mentions that it is a good idea to let the younger students know
what we think about a book or what it makes us think of, that it helps
to get a conversation going to also share our own responses. Gail
makes a mental note to teach a minilesson on how to handle the less
forthcoming younger children who often answer questions with a
shrug and "I don't know." She has noticed that several of the
younger students do this and decides that the class may benefit from
such a lesson. The debriefing session continues for a few more minutes, and then the class packs up for lunch. At lunchtime and during the week, the teachers meet to discuss their observations and
plan for the next buddy reading session.

## THE STUDENTS, THE SCHOOL,
## THE NEIGHBORHOOD

The students introduced in the pages of this book attend Hawthorne
Year-Round Elementary School in Oakland, California. The school is
huge by almost any standards. One thousand, three hundred students are enrolled and placed on one of four schedules. As three out
of the four schedules are in attendance at any time, approximately
one thousand students attend on any given day. What is now Hawthorne School used to be three schools—on the campus there are
three distinct school buildings which have been added to over the
years with portables.

Hawthorne is an inner-city school located in a low-income neighborhood that is home to many ethnic and immigrant groups. Large numbers of African Americans and first and second generation immigrants from Cambodia, El Salvador, Laos, Mexico, Nicaragua, and Vietnam live in the neighborhood. Smaller numbers of families are Chinese, European American, Filipino, Native American, and Pacific Islander.

Many of the students attending Hawthorne are acquiring English as a nonnative language. Some of the classes are designated as bilingual and teachers provide instruction in both English and Spanish. In other classes where many languages are spoken and the shared language is English, the teachers have received preparation in how to work with students acquiring English as a nonnative language. Gail and Mary fit within this latter category of teachers.

There are thirty first- and second-grade students in Mary's class, only nine of whom are girls. Their ethnic backgrounds vary: there are ten Laotians, six African Americans, five Vietnamese, three Chinese, two European Americans, two Mexicans, one Samoan, and one Tongan. About two-thirds of the students are in the process of learning English; the rest are fluent English speakers. English is the most dominant language, as that is the common language in the class, but many of the students speak Lao with each other.

Gail's fifth/sixth-grade class of thirty students is just as ethnically mixed. There are nine Laotians, six Mexicans, three African Americans, three El Salvadorans, two European Americans, two Native Americans, one Cambodian, one Chinese, one Fijian, one Filipino, and one Guatemalan. Again, English is the shared, common language in the class, but a third of the students speak Spanish and almost a third speak Lao. Gail's class has equal numbers of boys and girls.

When many of the students acquiring English speak, one can often detect evidence of the fact that English is not a native language for them. For example, you may notice in some of the excerpts of children's language the presence of reversed word order, the absence of articles, some confusion over pronouns and verb tenses, and apparent searches for appropriate words. These are typical developmental miscues from second language learners. We have reproduced the oral and written language of the students exactly as it occurred in order for readers to better know the students and their achievements. Many of the issues that we faced while implementing and maintaining a buddy reading program were related to working with students who are acquiring English as a nonnative language, and we will discuss them in greater detail later in the book (e.g., in Chapters 2 and 3).

We have included this background information in order for readers to realize that a successful buddy reading program is possible in circumstances that often seem very difficult. As educators of and advocates for all students, particularly those for whom other educators often have low expectations (e.g., inner-city students from low-income and/or immigrant backgrounds), we are constantly searching for effective ways to build upon the children's knowledge, experiences, interests, and special skills. We have come to realize that a well-designed buddy reading program can do just that.

## IN THE BEGINNING

The buddy reading program that we have just described did not come into existence overnight. In fact, it has taken six years for it to evolve. It also began rather uncertainly and unambitiously. Initially, Gail was concerned about one underachieving child, Gregory, a fifth grader who was not a fluent or experienced reader and could not read the literature that the rest of the class was reading. He also had a tendency to fight and bully other students, and had created a tough, intimidating image for himself that seemed to boost his confidence. Throughout the day, Gregory would call out negative comments and put down students, apparently as a way to disguise how he felt about his lack of academic success. In the year before joining Gail's class, he had spent over half of his time in the school office because of disruptive behavior. He told Gail that he was shocked that he had passed to fifth grade. She wondered, "What am I going to do with Gregory?"

Obviously, she couldn't put him in a second-grade class for reading, even though this was his "reading level." She thought about putting him in a second-grade class as a tutor in hopes that this would help him acquire the reading skills he lacked. In fact, Gregory went to Mary's second-grade class for two weeks. He read to individual second graders and played word games with them. The arrangement was successful for a short time, but Gregory began to wander around the room and bother other students when he visited Mary's classroom. His behavior became a problem. He also felt singled out and isolated from his peers. It became clear to Gail and Mary that the arrangement wasn't working out as they had hoped, and they came to the conclusion that Gregory had seen through their arrangement—in spite of their telling him that it was to help the second graders with their reading, he knew why he was being sent to the second-grade class and seemed to rebel.

Gail had other students with similar academic and interpersonal problems. She knew that they were frustrated by their lack of success in school and the fact that they were underachievers. The way in which they expressed this frustration demanded an inordinate amount of her attention and time. These students could barely read, and they weren't interested in being in school. They were unwilling to read materials that were at their independent reading level because they were embarrassed to be seen with "baby" books. Instead of reading picture books, they simply didn't read. Gail wondered how she was going to help these students. What should she do with them? It was at this point six years ago that the idea of a modified buddy reading program began to evolve. Gail and Mary decided to pair up several students in each class and have them read to each other. In this way Gregory and the other fifth graders wouldn't feel singled out while getting the kind of practice with print that they needed. Many of Gail's students were struggling readers and she realized that they could benefit from the practice of reading to a younger buddy.

This difficult experience with some older, under-achieving students with "behavior problems" was the motivation for Gail to embark on a buddy reading program several years ago. She wanted to provide her struggling readers with successful reading experiences that would enhance their views of themselves as readers. This first attempt at what was later to be "Buddy Reading" was actually a way to give a few fifth graders in Gail's class opportunities to read at their independent reading level. So, despite the mixed results with the experiment with Gregory, Gail went back to Mary with another request. Would Mary be willing to let a few of Gail's fifth graders read to some of her first graders? Mary agreed and a small-scale buddy reading program was launched.

And the plan worked! The first graders idolized the upper grade students, not noticing that their older buddies struggled as readers. The older students were focused and engaged. Mary had been concerned that she would have discipline problems with Gail's students, but this was never an issue. The older students didn't seem to realize that in the process of reading to the younger students, they were actually reading, something they dreaded, if not hated, doing. In fact, they enjoyed the stories and the reading immensely, and waited with great anticipation for each session. Mary and Gail were so impressed with the success of this exchange that they wondered if they should do it with all their students. There was further motivation to expand the program as Gail was still concerned that the older students involved would eventually feel stigmatized. Mary saw advantages for her own students as many of the younger students did not have anyone at home to read to them in English. She saw the possibility for every child to be read to individually on a regular basis. So the two teachers sat down after school one afternoon and began pairing up their students.

It seemed so easy. They explained to the older students that half of the first/second-grade class would exchange places with half of their class. Each student would have a special buddy and they would read, write, and draw together. Both classes were told that the older buddies would help the younger buddies practice their reading and writing. The teachers explained that Mary had thirty students and didn't have enough time to work individually with each child as often as she would like. Therefore, the older students would work with a buddy once a week.

Sometimes there were logistical problems that impeded the progress of the program. For example, Gail and Mary taught in two entirely different buildings which meant that the younger students had to be picked up and escorted back to Gail's class. It would take ten minutes at the beginning and another ten minutes at the end of the session to complete this exchange. Also, they teach in a multi-track, year-round school where students and teachers are on four different schedules, known as sixty/twenty. This means that they are in school for sixty days then out on intersession for twenty days. This gives each schedule three, one-month breaks over the course of a year. Every month a different schedule goes out on vacation. In those early days of buddy reading, Gail and Mary were not on the same schedule. In fact, they had schedules with back-to-back vacations, which presented a problem as one class would return from a month's vacation just as the other class was about to leave for its month-long break. Consequently, students would not see their buddies for two months at a stretch. It was very disjointed.

That crazy schedule was also a blessing in disguise, however, as it gave the teachers feedback from the students, who were constantly asking when their buddies would be back from vacation: "Will they be back next week?" "Is next week buddy reading?" "When are we having buddy reading?" Mary and Gail began to get a sense of how important buddy reading was to the students. It thrilled them, and they felt that they had stumbled onto something. The results far exceeded their original expectations and goals. As Mary and Gail talked, they began to understand what was going on. Buddy reading was a very important part of their students' lives. They realized that the program was having a very positive influence on the older children's reading development and attitudes. It was also enhancing the development of their social skills as they learned how to interact successfully with others. Gail and Mary also realized that they needed to make some structural changes if they were going to be able to sustain the program. By the end of the first year, they knew that they needed to be on the same schedule. It took two years of negotiating with the principal, but three years ago they were placed on the same schedule. And being on the same schedule did make a difference as the students knew with some certainty that they would meet with their buddies each week.

The predictable weekly meetings were critical to the students viewing buddy reading as a serious and integral part of their school program. The younger students got into a rhythm, looked forward to, and planned for their weekly meetings. As the younger students became more accustomed to the routine of buddy reading, it became a positive force in their lives. As they became more comfortable with their buddies, they began taking more risks. For example, they were less hesitant to speak up during shared reading, and were more likely to make predictions when confronted by unknown words.

The success of the buddy reading program is undoubtedly related to the fact that both Gail and Mary share a similar philosophy of and approach to teaching. Over the years, both teachers have moved steadily away from the traditional, teacher-centered, skills-based instructional strategies that characterized their teacher preparation programs and early teaching experiences. They began to abandon reading textbooks in favor of children's literature that had been written to entertain and inform young readers, and they found that this change transformed their previously disinterested students; it also transformed how excited they felt about teaching. Mary introduced her students to shared reading, which is grounded in the work of New Zealand educators Marie Clay and Don Holdaway, who carefully observed the literacy processes of young children (see Clay 1982; Holdaway 1979). It is characterized by children reading and re-reading "real" books (trade books) that often have predictable, repetitive elements. While becoming familiar with the rhythm and rhyme of familiar and favorite books, poems, chants, and songs, children also learn about the structure of language. Children read stories together, often sharing an enlarged version (big books).

Several years ago, Gail abandoned her reading contracts and class sets of literature and introduced *literature study circles,* an approach to reading development that emphasizes reading and discussing unabridged, unexcerpted children's literature (see Eeds & Wells 1989; Edelsky 1988; Peterson & Eeds 1990; Samway, et al. 1991). Students who have read the same text meet with the teacher after a few days to discuss the book. Discussions, which follow the reading of a complete text, are open-ended, rather than being artificially led/directed by the teacher. Both the students and the teacher are knowledgeable learners in these discussions, which generally explore both personal responses to and literary features of the book.

After a few months with the more successful buddy reading program, Mary and Gail decided to integrate art and cooking into the program. These were two areas where some of the less academically successful students were very talented and could show off their expertise. About once a month, following a half hour reading and writing session, the younger students would receive individual help in completing an art or crafts project (e.g., making haunted houses, snowflakes, three-dimensional spring flowers, and painting using Monart, an art technique). Although all the students worked on their own projects, the older students would supervise and guide their younger buddies. When it came to cooking, Ms. Phoutaboum, an instructional assistant, would take three pairs of students each week to cook in the school's kitchen. Everybody enjoyed eating the Vietnamese noodle soup, tacos, Laotian egg rolls, buñuelos and brownies that the cooks brought back to the classrooms each week.

The students looked forward to the art and crafts activities and cooking experiences. They offered the students opportunities to work together in different ways. Students who had artistic talent were able to shine and demonstrate this to their buddies. The art and crafts projects also filled a gap that one sometimes finds in the intermediate grades. Whereas primary students are often engaged in hands-on activities and art projects, this happens less and less as the students progress through the upper grades. This addition to buddy reading provided the older students with opportunities to express themselves in less common ways. It also provided them with immediate and concrete success as their products were noticeably more sophisticated than those of their younger buddies. All of the students celebrated in their creations. Fabulous cut-away haunted houses hung from clothes-lines in the two classrooms. Intricate snowflakes hung delicately around the room and complicated three-dimensional flowers stood tall and colorful in the middle of every table.

In previous years, while the students met together, Gail and Mary would occasionally walk around their rooms, but for the most part they sat at their desks and read papers, cleaned up the mess that accumulates in any classroom, or prepared for the next part of the day. In a sense, it was free time for the teachers. The students were all involved, so Gail and Mary felt that the program was a success. It did not occur to them then that so much more could be done with buddy reading. Their roles took a new direction over a year ago, though, after a visit from Katharine Davies Samway, a teacher-educator at a local university. She and Gail had been working together on developing a literature-based reading program, which involved weekly visits to the fifth/sixth-grade class during their language arts block . However, on this day a slight scheduling change resulted in her observing a buddy reading session. She saw how transformed many of the older children were by the experience.

Even the toughest children were nurturing with their buddies. The usually reserved students were invigorated and dynamic. She noticed how some of the children exhibited extraordinary talent as teachers . . . patient, supportive, and enthusiastic. In the debriefing session, she heard how proud they were of their younger buddies' accomplishments, and how they felt that they were making a significant contribution to their buddies' development as readers. She also heard the problems they experienced (e.g., inattentive buddies, buddies not being able to read or write) and realized that although they didn't know much about emerging literacy, they were ripe for instruction in how to work with younger learners. Katharine began to visit the fifth- and sixth-grade class as a participant/observer during the weekly buddy reading sessions. She became the extra pair of ears and eyes that helped Gail and Mary extend and fine-tune what they had been working on for a long time.

When Katharine first started to visit each week during buddy reading, she worked exclusively in Gail's class, and focused primarily on the older buddies, the tutors. We hadn't realized then how important it is to also work intensively with the younger children. This became apparent to us one day when Gail and Jenny Rienzo, a student from a local college who was helping us collect data, were providing Katharine with feedback on a draft of an article that she was writing. Jenny pointed out that most of the emphasis was on the older children. It was only then, when Jenny made this comment, that we realized that we needed to be working more closely with Mary. For our next meeting, we asked Mary to join us, and it was at this point that we began to collaborate very closely.

Although the teachers' primary responsibility during buddy reading was to manage the whole class, Gail and Mary began to take on another role, one of observer. At the beginning, it was difficult for them to move into this different role and not revert back to the teacher-as-manager role. At first, they resisted the idea of keeping notes as they moved around their classrooms, believing that they would be distracted or that they wouldn't be able to both observe, write notes, and also be aware of what was going on throughout the room. Once they realized, however, that they didn't have to write the detailed or continuous kinds of notes that Katharine was keeping, Mary and Gail began to carefully and more systematically watch and listen to the interactions that flowed around them. They found that they could learn a great deal from these two- to three-minute focused observations of a child or buddy pair . . . and still oversee the whole class. In this way, they became better attuned to the accomplishments and needs of their students.

At lunchtime, following the buddy reading experience, we would all meet to discuss our findings and plan for future sessions. Whereas before, Mary and Gail communicated to each other about the program, but essentially ran two independent programs, now we began to work together to prepare for one program that was housed in two classrooms. The teachers had questions about the program and students which they asked Katharine and Jenny to focus on in their observations and notetaking. For example, on more than one occasion sixth grader Vanessa had commented in debriefing sessions that her partner, Margaret, was not easy to work with and didn't "want to learn." Gail asked Katharine and Jenny to spend time observing this partnership. Their sustained observations over two weeks revealed that Margaret was actually quite engaged and keen to show off her emerging reading prowess. However, Vanessa seemed impatient with Margaret's inability to "read properly" and displayed her frustration through shrugs, loud sighs, ignoring Margaret's questions and comments, and constantly correcting the younger girl's approximations, all of which seemed to result in Margaret losing confidence in herself. We realized that Gail needed to address with her class effective ways of supporting emerging readers.

Fieldnotes also sparked discussions, which then led to instructional decisions. For example, Katharine had been observing Richard and Sammy reading a science magazine, which Sammy had carefully selected one day after the buddy reading session had begun. It had clearly been a frustrating experience for Richard as he had tried to read all the words surrounding the photographs and had a lot of difficulty doing that. Eventually Sammy got distracted and Richard became impatient with him. It occurred to us as we discussed Katharine's fieldnotes that it would be a good idea for Gail to lead a minilesson on how to read aloud nonfiction books and magazines, which she did the next week. In this way, instructional decisions and questions influenced what we focused on when observing the students, and observations influenced instructional and management decisions. That is, a symbiotic relationship evolved in which observations and instructional and management decisions influenced each other.

We have collaborated in closely observing buddy reading sessions and learning from what we have heard and seen. We have witnessed compelling growth in the students as learners and teachers. Our observations have guided us, in the kinds of questions we have asked, in what we have taught, and in how we have set up and managed the buddy reading sessions. We have learned a great deal from the experience and from talking with other teachers who have implemented buddy reading programs. We have also learned a lot from reading about cross-age tutoring programs (e.g., Heath & Mangiola 1991; Juel 1991; Labbo & Teale 1990; Leland & Fitzpatrick 1994; Morrice & Simmons 1991). We have made mistakes and tried to learn from those mistakes, and our learning continues through the writing of this book. It has been an odyssey. It is the story of this odyssey and what we have learned from it that we would like to share in the remainder of the book.

# 2

## "That's Not How You Spell Breakfast!"

## Initial Preparation for a Buddy Reading Program

As teachers, we often hear about cross-age tutoring programs at workshops and conferences, in professional magazines, and in the faculty room. We may be excited by the success stories that we hear and read about, and vow to implement such a program immediately. However, despite our good intentions, many cross-age tutoring programs die a quiet death almost as soon as they are introduced. In some cases, it is because the two teachers are not equally committed to the program and do not spend much time sharing and planning. Sometimes the teachers have radically different philosophies of teaching, which lead to conflicts. In other cases, the tutoring sessions are viewed as free time and become chaotic. In yet other cases, the children lose their enthusiasm because they do not understand the purpose of the program or their respective roles. Successful programs can be thrilling. But successful buddy reading programs also need commitment from all the people involved as well as a lot of on-going thought, planning, and preparation. Successful programs do not appear overnight, as in a fairy tale.

Before the students ever work together, a great deal of preparation is necessary if the experience is to have a chance to succeed. We have found that it is particularly successful if we spend about one month preparing the students. Also, as teachers we need this time to prepare. We should stress that throughout the year we often need to return to the same issues that we initially addressed before the program got off the ground.

## PREPARING OURSELVES
## FOR BUDDY READING

When we first started the cross-age buddy reading program, we just jumped into it and then found that we had to backtrack a lot. We have since discovered that the program runs more smoothly if we spend time in the beginning working closely together to prepare ourselves, our students, and our classrooms. We have found it very helpful to focus on the following:

1. *Observe students more carefully and frequently* in order to become acutely aware of their language, literacy, and interpersonal skills and needs. These observations have been very helpful when pairing up students. For example, we noticed that María, a fifth grader who was very reserved in small group discussions that occurred in English, was an animated leader when the discussions were in Spanish. We used this knowledge when it came time to select a partner for her, and paired her with Enrique, a child who was fully bilingual (equally fluent in English and Spanish), so María would be able to use her dominant language while working with her buddy.

2. *Consult with each other about children's literature* that the younger children enjoy. This has meant that other teachers, including Mary and Katharine, have become expert resources to Gail, who has become knowledgeable about easy reading books, big books, predictable books, wordless books, nonfiction picture books, and children's magazines intended for the primary grades. Now Gail is much more familiar with popular authors and illustrators of children's picture books, and is able to make informed recommendations to her fifth- and sixth-grade students.

   One dilemma that we have faced and have only recently begun to address to our satisfaction is finding books for emerging readers that reflect the diverse cultures that are represented at Hawthorne School and within the United States. Most of the predictable books or books with shorter texts that have been so successful with the buddy readers have characters that are predominantly of European descent. Publishers are beginning to publish more books for young readers that are set in and explore issues that are grounded in diverse communities, which has made our quest a little easier.

3. *Create a primary-grade library in the upper-grade classroom* so that the older students will have immediate access to appropriate books and magazines. Gail has extended her fifth-/sixth-grade library in various ways. She has borrowed books from friends and colleagues, checked out books from the school's book room and library, raided Mary's classroom, used book club bonus points to purchase picture books, and brought in books and magazines from her home collection. Whenever the occasion arises, she writes small grants to stock

her shelves with more books and magazines. Gail is now in the process of establishing with her students a system for organizing and storing these books (e.g., on display shelves, book shelves, and in plastic baskets). She is doing it this way because, in the past, when the students were not involved in the process, books were shelved randomly. Later, students couldn't find what they were looking for, which led to a lot of random selection of books, many of which were not appropriate for the younger buddies.

## PREPARING THE STUDENTS FOR BUDDY READING

We have found that it is critical to spend several weeks intensively preparing the students for the buddy reading experience. Although much of the preparation focuses on the older students as they are the teachers, it is equally important to pay attention to the younger learners. We will first address what we do when preparing the older students and then discuss how we prepare the younger children. Please see Figures 1 and 2 for an overview of the month-long preparation that we recently gave the fifth/sixth and first/second graders respectively.

---

When preparing the older students for the most recent buddy reading program, we engaged in the following activities:

*Early September:*
- Buddy reading concept introduced. Sixth graders shared experiences from the previous year. Mary introduced why she wanted fifth-/sixth-grade buddy readers.
- Students introduced to children's literature for young children. Gail modeled by reading several picture books which class discussed.
- Children began to read and evaluate fifty books.
- Small group meetings held weekly to discuss favorite books and authors.
- Gail assessed her students' reading and writing ability.

*Late September:*
- Groups of students observed Mary during story time and discussed observations.
- Students continued reading children's literature for young children.
- Gail and Mary met to pair up buddies.
- Minilessons conducted (e.g., on read-aloud and questioning strategies, developmental stages of reading and writing, how to hold a book, using pictures to retell a story).
- Gail and Mary met to plan a method for students to meet their buddies.

---

FIGURE 1   *Schedule for the initial preparation of fifth and sixth graders.*

When preparing the younger students for the most recent buddy reading program, we engaged in the following activities:
*Early September:*
- Children engaged in sustained silent reading for twenty minutes each day during the reading block.
- Children read with and to an adult on a regular basis once or twice a week.
- Mary assessed each child's reading and writing ability.

*Late September:*
- Students continued to engage in daily silent reading.
- Students continued to read to an adult on a regular basis.
- Minilessons conducted (e.g., on attentive listening, selecting books, how to have a discussion).
- Class discussed the idea of buddy reading. Second graders from last year talked about their experiences.
- Mary and Gail met to match up students.
- Mary and Gail met to plan the first meeting between buddies.

FIGURE 2    *Schedule for the initial preparation of first and second graders.*

## Preparing the Older Students for Buddy Reading

We have found it helpful to focus on the following elements when working with the older students.

**Purposes of the buddy reading program.** When we first started buddy reading a few years ago, we neglected to explain thoroughly the purposes of the program. Although it was successful and both groups of children enjoyed the cross-age experience, we did not realize then its potential for developing the language and literacy of all the students. Just as we are better teachers when we know why we are doing what we do, so it is with these younger teachers. We now realize the importance of letting the older students know exactly why they are being prepared to work with the younger group of children whose classroom is across the patio.

Gail used to explain the goals of the program to her fifth/sixth grade students, but we have discovered that it is more authentic and successful for Mary to come to the upper grade classroom and explain how important it is for emerging readers and writers to be read to every day . . . and to have the opportunity to read to another person on a regular basis. She explains that it is impossible for her to listen and read to her students as often as she would like, and is looking forward to their help in meeting her goals as a teacher. She then goes on to explain that reading aloud, writing with, and interacting with young children is not always easy and that we are going to teach them how to do it more successfully.

**Studying children's literature that is appropriate for use with the younger learners.** For many of the fifth and sixth graders, it has been several years since they have read picture books and they often do not know what is available or how authors' and illustrators' styles of writing and illustrating vary. In order to be able to make successful selections, the students need to be intimately familiar with a variety of fiction and nonfiction literature, particularly books that the younger children are familiar with and enjoy. In preparation for buddy reading, the students read many children's books, and discuss the books with their peers and Gail. To begin with, Gail reads a picture book to her class on a daily basis, followed by a class discussion. In a recent conversation about *The Nine Days of Camping* (Williams 1990), a predictable book modeled on The *Twelve Days of Christmas* (Brett 1988), the discussion focused on how predictable elements help emerging readers:

GAIL: What did you notice about this book? [pause]
ROBERTO: I knew what was gonna' happen next.
ESMERALDA:  It was like a song.
ANGELINA: I can guess the next part.
GAIL: Oh, have you read this book before?
STUDENTS: No.
GAIL: Then how did you know what was gonna' happen next?
ROBERTO: 'Cuz it keep on repeating.
GAIL: This is what we call a predictable book. It's really helpful for beginning readers because they can predict the words that may come next.

The class continued to explore the different ways in which books can be predictable and how pictures are often integral to this predictable quality in many children's books.

During the first month, Gail allocates about thirty minutes three times a week for the students in her class to read picture books. Many of the books take the children only a couple of minutes to read (e.g., *The Birthday Cake* [Cowley 1987a], *Snowy Day* [Keats 1987], *Peter's Chair* [Keats 1983], and big books), whereas others may take them much longer (e.g., *Cloudy With A Chance of Meatballs* [Barrett 1978], *Rumpelstiltskin* [Galdone 1985]). The students discover authors who are popular with Mary's class. They also develop their own list of favorite authors—Leo Lionni, Eric Carle, Dr. Seuss, and Arnold Lobel have become some of their favorites. Books written by these authors are usually easy to read and many have predictable texts. When the students explain why these authors are their favorites, they are likely to mention that Eric Carle writes about animals in a humorous way, Dr. Seuss books are longer but still predictable, and Leo Lionni's books have beautiful illustrations. Before meeting with their buddies, the fifth- and sixth-grade students must read fifty books that are appropriate for the younger children so that they will become familiar with books that are available, become knowledgeable about different authors and genres, and start to develop their own read-aloud preferences. They record the books they read on a Buddy Reading Booklist, which includes the title, author, genre, some brief comments and a rating of the book. See Figure 3 for an

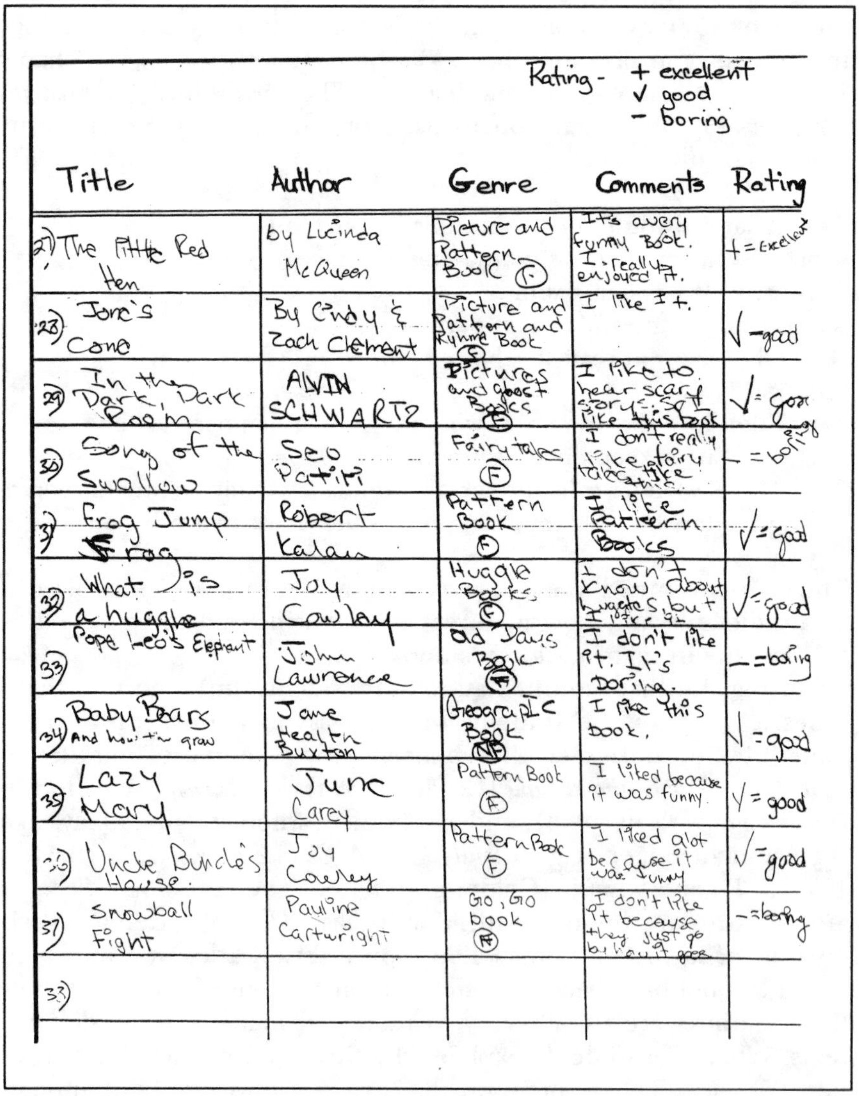

Rating - + excellent
√ good
− boring

| Title | Author | Genre | Comments | Rating |
|---|---|---|---|---|
| 27) The Little Red Hen | by Lucinda McQueen | Picture and Pattern Book (F) | It's a very funny Book. I really enjoyed it. | + = Excellent |
| 28) Jone's Cone | By Cindy & Zach Clement | Picture and Pattern and Ryhme Book (F) | I like It. | √ = good |
| 29) In the Dark, Dark Room | ALVIN SCHWARTZ | Pictures and ghost Books (F) | I like to hear scary storys. So I like this book | √ = good |
| 30) Song of the Swallow | Seo Patiri | Fairy tales (F) | I don't really like fairy tales like this | − = boring |
| 31) Frog Jump Frog | Robert Kalan | Pattern Book (F) | I like Pattern Books | √ = good |
| 32) What is a huggle | Joy Cowley | Huggle Books (F) | I don't know about huggles, but I like it | √ = good |
| 33) Pope Leo's Elephant | John Lawrence | Old Days Book (F) | I don't like it. It's boring. | − = boring |
| 34) Baby Bears And how they grow | Jane Health Buxton | GeograpIC Book (NF) | I like this book. | √ = good |
| 35) Lazy Mary | June Carey | Pattern Book (F) | I liked because it was funny. | √ = good |
| 36) Uncle Buncle's House | Joy Cowley | Pattern Book (F) | I liked a lot because it was funny | √ = good |
| 37) Snowball Fight | Pauline Cartwright | Go, Go book (F) | I don't like it because they just go by how it goes. | − = boring |
| 38) | | | | |

FIGURE 3 *An excerpt from Choulaphone's booklist.*

excerpt from Choulaphone's booklist. This record helps the students select books and make book recommendations once they have begun to tutor the first and second graders.

**Responding to books.** The older students already have experience talking with each other about more extended texts through engaging in literature study circles (e.g., Peterson & Eeds 1990; Samway, et al. 1991), but they have not had much experience discussing shorter texts and texts with a lot of pictures. They often need practice in how to talk about books written for younger learners so, after the students have read approximately ten books, they bring their favorite books to small group discussions where they share aspects of the books that interested them. The discussions frequently cover a wide range of issues including plot, illustrations, predictability of the text, genre, theme, and the author/illustrator's style of writing/ illustrating. We have noticed that the children especially enjoy reading humorous books with predictable elements and engaging illustrations (e.g., Judith Viorst's *Alexander and the Terrible, Horrible, No Good, Very Bad Day* [1976]). Following the discussion, the children briefly brainstorm other books, authors, genres, and themes that they're interested in reading for the next weekly small group book discussions. The older students seem to be better prepared for a discussion with the younger children if they have been given opportunities to talk about picture books with their peers.

**Read-aloud strategies.** The way we read to others can have a profound impact on how our listeners respond. For example, if we read fluently, altering our speed, volume, and tone to reflect different characters and changes in the plot, we are more likely to engage our listeners. In order to become more skilled at reading aloud, the fifth and sixth graders visit Mary's class in groups of six or seven to observe her conducting a read-aloud. Gail prepares her students by asking them to notice how Mary reads the book. In order not to overwhelm them, she suggests that the groups focus on only one element each time they visit, such as:

1. Does the teacher read the book without stopping? Is there any conversation? What does the conversation focus on?
2. How does the teacher handle interruptions?
3. How does the teacher act during read aloud? Does she laugh or make any comments?
4. How does the teacher keep the attention of the students?
5. How and when does the teacher vary her voice?
6. What questions does the teacher ask her students?

The teachers coordinate these observations so that, before the students observe a read-aloud during storytime, they are already familiar with the story. In this way, the students can focus on read-aloud strategies rather than the story itself. As they watch and listen, they take notes. For example, Tamara observed Mary reading *Who Took the Farmer's Hat?* (Nodset 1963). Gail had suggested that the group of fifth and sixth graders focus on questions asked by the teacher during the read-aloud. Tamara wrote the following entry in her log:

> What do you think this is going to be about? Let's look in the pic-
> ture. What's happing. So the title of this story is. Get relaxed. Do
> you see that _____ ? Do you have something like that? Where
> do you thinks it's going to go? Driffent vocies. Did you see the
> hat? So the _____ thought it was _____ . What does the_____
> do with it? What do you think it does? What kind of person is the
> _____ ?

It is clear from Tamara's use of dashes that she understood that her job was to observe general types of questions.

On Friday, the whole class meets together to discuss their obser-vations, using their fieldnotes to jog their memories. Recently, Gail asked the class to reflect upon the kinds of questions that Mary asked her students. The discussion covered a variety of topics, but Gail selected just a few to explore in greater depth, as the following excerpt illustrates:

GAIL: What questions did you hear Ms. Pippitt ask her students during her story time? [pause]
TAMARA: She ask if anyone has read the book before.
BARBARA: She ask, "What do you think is gonna happen in the story?"
DAMLONGSONG: Who your favorite character?
CHOULAPHONE: I hear her say, "Did you like this story?"
GAIL: Why do you think Ms. Pippitt asked, "What do you think is gonna happen?"
JOSH: She's trying to get them excited about the book so they'll pay attention when she's reading it.
GAIL: Uh huh. What else?
LANCE: She want to know if they read the book before.
GAIL: Asking students to predict, like Ms. Pippitt did, is a good way to get your buddy interested and involved in the story. This is a good strat-egy before beginning the book. I wouldn't use it before every page because it breaks the flow of the story.

Through a brief discussion such as this, Gail is able to introduce her students to concrete teaching strategies.

**Gaining familiarity with the developmental nature of reading and writing.** Sometimes we have observed older buddies criticizing the attempts of first and second graders to read and write, and this has concerned us. For example, one of the more struggling sixth-grade readers, Richard, sometimes reprimanded his buddy, Sammy, for not reading the words as printed on the page. "That's not what it say," he would remind Sammy, as if remembering how often he had been told in remedial reading classes that reading means focusing on letters and sounds. On one occasion when Sammy was retelling a familiar story, *Green Eggs and Ham* (Seuss 1960), Amphaivane, who was sitting at the same table as Richard and Sammy, leaned over and said, "He can read?!" with an admiring tone in her voice. Richard quickly responded, "He can read *some* of them [the words]," sighed deeply, as if exasperated, and tersely interrupted with, "What about 'green eggs and ham'?" when Sammy did not say those words in the appropriate place. We realized that Richard, as well as the other children, probably did not know much about early reading and writing development. This was almost certainly complicated by the fact that what we valued as teachers when interacting with the younger students (e.g., making meaning, making predictions, and using phonics to confirm or disconfirm those predictions) was almost certainly at odds with what Richard, the struggling reader, had been taught over the years (e.g., focusing on making letter/sound correspondences and word by word reading). We realized that we needed to teach the older students something about how emerging reading and writing can vary a great deal.

We now make sure that in the first month we introduce the older students to the developmental nature of reading and writing. Gail explains that learning to write and read is similar to learning how to walk. The class talks about what we do if babies fall over when taking a few tentative steps—instead of chastising them, we pick them up, congratulate them on their accomplishments, and encourage them as they continue walking. We don't say, "Bad baby!" The students understand the analogy and are receptive to the notion that learning to read and write takes time, and is a developmental process. In preparation for a recent discussion in the upper-grade class on how the younger students use many strategies when writing, we decided to use authentic examples of writing from the first/second-grade class. As the younger children were already engaged in a unit on foods, Mary asked them to write a response to the *oral* prompt, "What do you eat for breakfast?" She explained that we would share these pieces of writing with the older students who wanted to see how first and second graders write. From these responses, Mary created an overhead illustrating the developmental stages of spelling present in her class of thirty students (see Figure 4). Gail then used this overhead to introduce the concept of developmental (invented) spelling to her students. As the class read the messages, it was clear that the older students had much less difficulty understanding the writing than Gail! The class then talked about the consequences of not accepting the younger children's writing efforts:

Developmental Spelling

| | |
|---|---|
| Beginnings (Scribble/Pictures | I L— |
| Consonants | IATSFB |
| Initial and Final Consonants | I at cl nd mk. |
| vowel/Consonant Combination | I at cero and milk it was good |
| Words | I ate soup fore breakfast and cerea and millk. |
| standard Spelling | I ate cereal and milk for breakfast. |

FIGURE 4 *Stages in developmental spelling.*

GAIL: How do you think your buddy would feel if you kept on saying, "No, that's not how you write 'meatball', that's not how you spell 'cloudy', that's not how you write 'rain'. 'Rain' has an 'i' in it"?

JUAN: I'd be mad.

RICHARD: He'd think he a bad speller.

ANGELINA: BAD. Real bad. He wouldn't want to write any more.

GAIL: Uh huh. Why not?

ANGELINA: Cuz you keep telling him he's doing it wrong and he wouldn't want to try any more.

VILIPHONE: They would keep asking you how to spell every word. To make sure they get it right. And that would be boring.

GAIL: Right. That's exactly why we don't correct them when they're writing. We want to encourage them to write. When they're first learning how to write, one of the first stages is to write the sounds they hear. Many of your buddies are at this stage. For example, this is how Mano writes "cloud" [*Gail writes CLD on the dry erase board*]. Now, some buddies are like Sammy and they aren't yet at that stage. He's just learning the sounds and he may write "C" for cloud, or he might use any letter like a "T" or an "L." It's important to support and encourage your buddies at whatever stage they're at in their writing.

Later in the week, after the students had been paired, the younger students wrote letters of introduction to their buddies. Many of the letters included information about names, ages, favorite TV shows, and pets. These letters sometimes consisted of developmental spelling (see Figure 5). Others contained fairly sophisticated conventional spelling (see Figure 6). Gail pointed out how the children are all writers in their own ways. After reading their letters, the fifth and sixth graders determined the developmental spelling stages of their buddies. We have found that this early preparation goes a long way towards avoiding uninformed criticisms, e.g., "That's not how you spell 'breakfast'."

For similar reasons, Gail also introduces her students to the range of reading strategies that their buddies may have access to. She remembers how, in a previous year, Richard and Amphaivane had reacted quite differently to the retelling of stories by their buddies based upon their familiarity with the texts. Richard had repeatedly chastised his buddy for not paying attention to the words and his buddy quickly lost interest in reading. In contrast, Amphaivane had been excited by what her buddy, Sung, was doing and constantly encouraged her; Sung proudly continued reading and commented later to Mary that Amphaivane had said she was a good reader.

The class explores with Gail how the younger children are likely to read using one or more of the following strategies, all of which are typical of emerging readers:

1. retelling a familiar story from memory, without reference to either text or pictures;
2. retelling a familiar story from memory, but using the pictures as a prompt;
3. using pictures to tell an unfamiliar story;
4. reading a familiar text word for word with some miscues;
5. reading an unfamiliar text with miscues;
6. reading fluently using context clues and phonics.

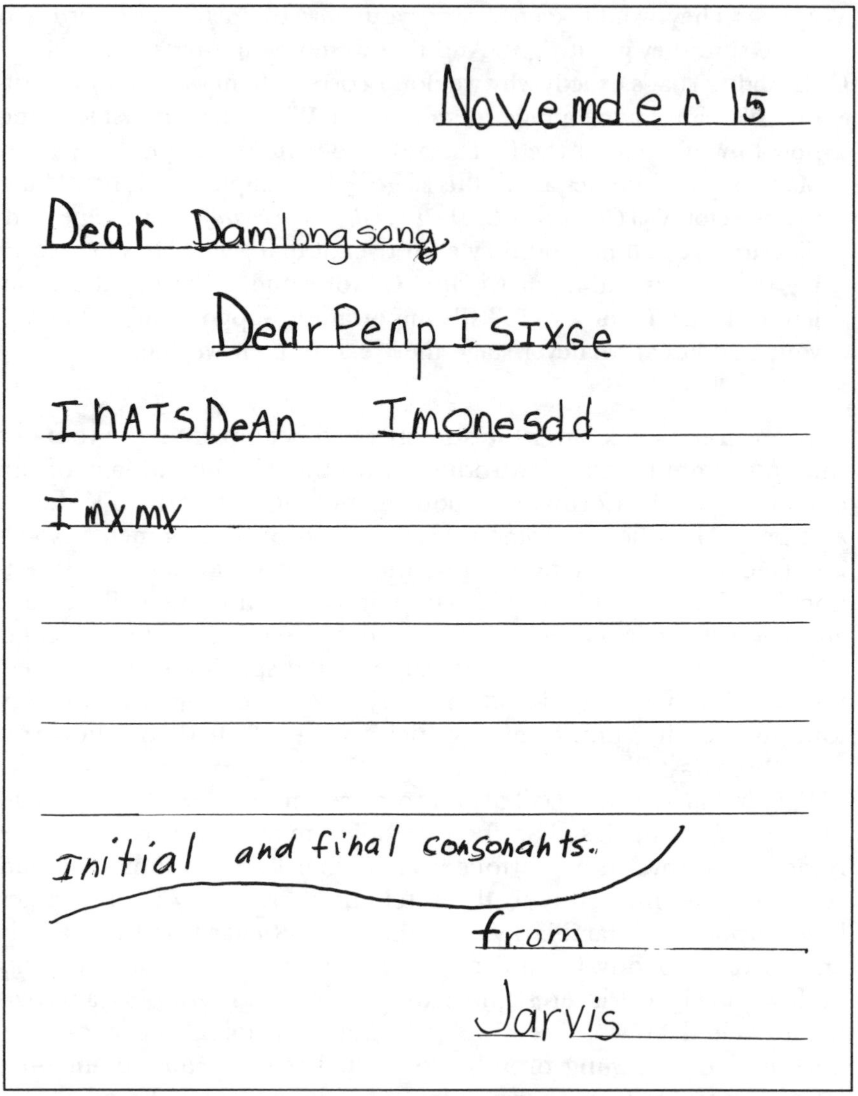

November 15

Dear Damlongsong,

    DearPenpISIXGe

IhATSDeAn    Imonesdd

Imxmx

Initial and final consonahts.

                    from

                    Jarvis

FIGURE 5    *Letter from a younger student using developmental spelling.*

We have found it helpful to share with the older students this type of developmental scale in order to validate what the younger students are doing when interacting with a text. We often introduce these stages with contrasting skits in which we demonstrate how some children who are the same age often read the same story very differently. Although we frequently use students to demonstrate points being addressed in these minilessons, at the beginning of the year we tend to rely on adults for the skits for two primary reasons: a) The two groups of students have not yet been paired at this time of the year and haven't had a chance to get to know and value each

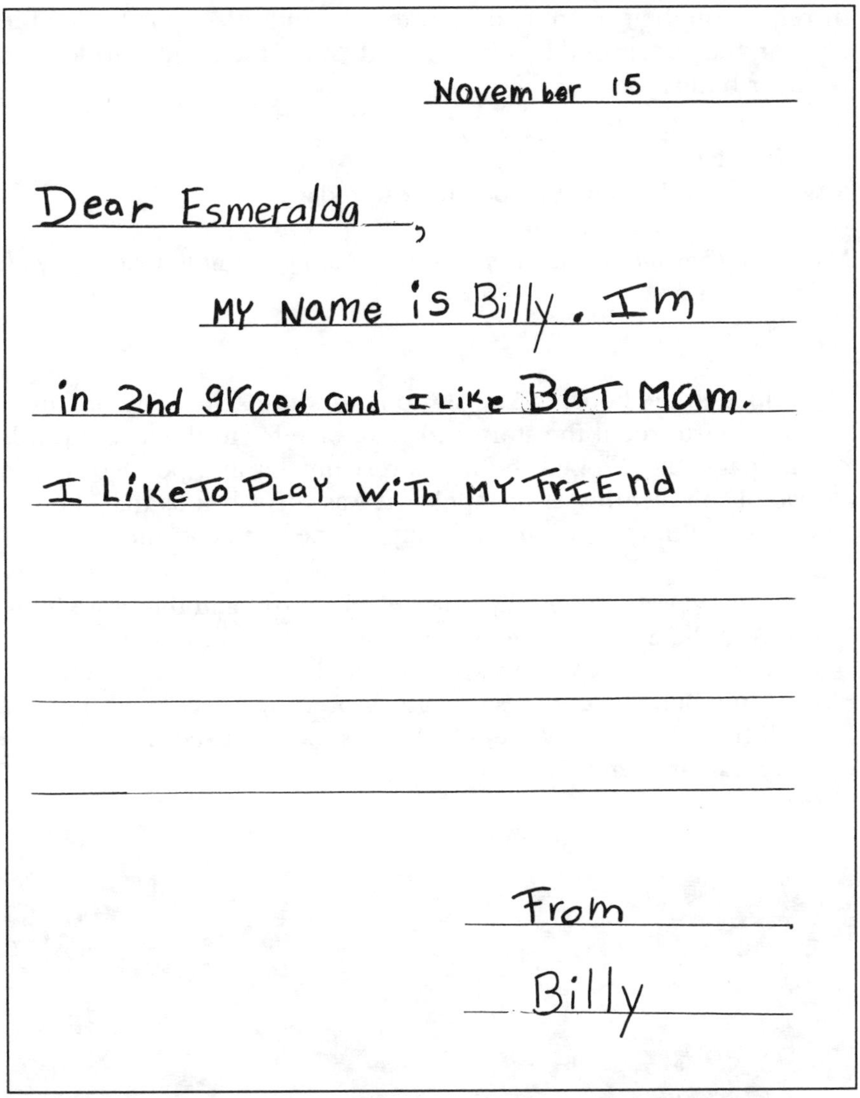

November 15

Dear Esmeralda___,

    My Name is Billy. I'm

in 2nd graed and I Like BaT Mam.

I LiKe To PLaY WiTh MY TriEnd

From

Billy

FIGURE 6   *Letter from a younger student using conventional spelling.*

other. We want to avoid the possibility of older students inadvertently making fun of the non-standardized oral reading of the younger children who may, for example, stumble over words or make up the text. b) We want to be sure that key points are addressed. If we demonstrate, we can ensure that points we wish to illustrate are made.

In a minilesson at the beginning of this year, on the day when the students were to read together for the first time, Gail and Mary demonstrated the need to support young readers who retell stories by relying on their memory of the story (see Photo 4). Gail acted the part of the older buddy/teacher and Mary took the part of the younger buddy:

GAIL: Hi, Mary.
MARY: Hi, Gail. I brought a book to read today.
GAIL: Great! What is it?
MARY: *The Three Billy Goats Gruff* [Galdone 1981]. I want to read it to you. Can I start now?
GAIL: Sure.

Mary opened the book and began to read with excitement. She used the pictures to retell the story and did not refer to the actual words on the page. She flipped the pages very quickly and pointed to one or two of the pictures as she spoke. It was very obvious that she was not actually referring to many, if any, of the words on the page:

> Once there were three Billy Goats named Gruff and they were hungry. And there was some grass and they wanted to eat it and that's the bridge. Trip trap, trip trap [using a high-pitched voice] went the Little Billy Goat. Who's that going over my bridge? said the Troll [in a deep, slow voice]. And that's the Troll and he's real mean and ugly . . .

PHOTO 4    *Mary and Gail role play during a minilesson.*

Gail's face showed obvious confusion during Mary's retelling and eventually she interrupted:

GAIL: No, Mary, no. That says, "'Who's that tripping over my bridge?' roared the Troll." You need to look at the words on the page. You're just looking at the pictures.
MARY: Oh yeah, I forgot. [She shrugs her shoulders and continues] And here's the Big Billy Goat and he says, trip trap, trip trap [Using a deep, slow voice].
GAIL: Mary, I told you to read the words on the page. It says, "Trip, trap, trip trap! went the bridge." [Gail's voice is now very irritated. There is a pause.]
MARY: You read now. [Mary is clearly dejected.]
GAIL: No, you read. You said that you wanted to read this story.
MARY: I can't read anymore. I've got a stomach ache. [She turns her face away, hunches her shoulders and crosses her arms over her stomach.]
GAIL: You don't know how to read, do you? I thought you said you could read?
MARY: I can but I don't want to right now.

When Gail and Mary had finished this skit, they asked the class to reflect upon what they had observed:

GAIL: What's happening here? Think about what you saw and heard. Let's go around the class and share what you saw happening.
AMPHAIVANE: You put her down.
RICHARD: You made her feel bad.
GAIL: What do you mean, Richard?
RICHARD: Well . . . you told her she don't read good.
VILIPHONE: She was excited at the beginning, but not at the end. You're not a good buddy. I wouldn't want you for my buddy! [She grins]
GAIL: Why do you say that, Viliphone?
VILIPHONE: 'Cuz you keep interrupting her and tell her what she do wrong. I think she feel bad. I would, too.

The students commented on how Gail's behavior had not supported Mary, whose enthusiasm had dwindled to the point of her being unwilling to continue reading. The discussion continued to explore how Gail had undermined Mary:

GAIL: What did you see me doing that caused Ms. Pippitt to lose interest in reading?
JUAN: You keep interrupting her.
SOHEILA: You said, "No, no, that's not what it says."
JOSH: She was reading the book, Ms. Whang, but you kept telling her she wasn't.

GAIL: But she wasn't reading the words, Josh. What do you mean, she was reading the book?

JOSH: You don't have to read all the words to read. My little brother can't read all the words, but he can read.

GAIL: Exactly. Telling a story using the pictures and your memory of the story is one way that beginning readers read and we need to encourage them. Ms. Pippitt and I want to show you now how we can support our buddies who may not yet be able to read the words, but are excited about books and that's what we need to encourage.

We decided to re-enact the same scenario but with Gail playing the part of a supportive buddy. Mary left the circle and re-entered as an enthusiastic first-grade reader:

MARY: Hi, Gail. I brought my favorite book to read.

GAIL: Great! What did you bring today?

MARY: *The Three Billy Goats Gruff.* Can I read it to you?

GAIL: Sure, that's one of my favorites, too. I remember when my teacher read it to me when I was in first grade.

Mary opened the book and began to retell the story in the same way she began in the earlier skit. Whenever Mary chanted predictable elements, e.g., the refrain, "trip trap, trip trap," Gail joined in. Once Mary had finished reading, Gail commented:

GAIL: Good, Mary. I can see you really like this book. You're a good reader!' [Mary's face lights up in a huge smile.]

MARY: I have this book at home, you know. I read it every night to my sister.

GAIL: How come it's your favorite book?

MARY: 'Cuz I like the ugly troll in the book.

GAIL: What do you like about him?

MARY: He's got yellow teeth like my brother [both laugh].

GAIL: I like this book, too. I like the way I can change my voice when I'm reading about the different characters. This weekend I went on a hike with my family and we walked over a wooden bridge and pretended to be billy goats! My son, Daniel, was the troll. We had so much fun.

MARY: I like to be the troll, too, and my sister pretends to be the little billy goat.

The skit ended at this point and once again Gail invited the class to reflect upon what they had observed:

GAIL: What happened this time? How was it different?

TAMARA: You told her she was a good reader. You made her feel proud.

MARÍA: You are muy simpática. You tell her she a good reader.

PAUL: You encouraged her and read with her. Like with "trip trap, trip trap."

CHOULAPHONE: You told her that you liked the book and about your family goin' over a bridge like the billy goats.

GAIL: How did Mary feel this time?

TAMARA: She felt proud of herself.

AMPHAIVANE: She think she reading the book.

JESÚS: She smiled and was happy.

GAIL: OK. So, let's summarize what we learned today about how we work with our buddies when they're beginning readers and may not yet know how to read the words on the page.

As the students generated insights, Mary wrote key points on chart paper:

1. Give encouragements when your buddy is reading.
2. Let them read.
3. Don't tell them they don't know how to read.
4. It's OK to tell the story in your own words.
5. Tell your opinion about the book.

Gail drew upon an experience from the previous year to illustrate the impact of supporting young readers and writers.

GAIL: Today when you read with your buddy, remember what you learned today. Last year, I remember Malcolm brought in a book called *Rain* [Kaplan 1978] and he didn't know how to read it. He would look at the pictures and say, "It's a yellow sun, it's a blue sky, it's a brown fence" and he was just reading the pictures and Jesús would look up at me and knowingly smile and say, "Good, Malcolm, you can read." It gave him so much confidence. Jesús wasn't concerned that Malcolm couldn't read the words. He accepted the fact that at this stage in Malcolm's development as a reader, he was just reading the pictures.

MARY: Yes, Malcolm really was encouraged and he loved to read and this year he's reading on his own. He's so proud of himself. Jesús helped Malcolm become a reader.

Since providing initial orientation to the developmental nature of reading and writing, we have noticed that the older students are much more supportive of their buddies. We frequently hear the fifth and sixth graders encouraging their younger buddies with comments like, "Good," or "You're a good reader." They excitedly share with Gail what their buddy is reading and constantly reflect on the younger child's developmental stage in reading. Angelina commented, "Today I discovered that my buddy knows the sounds of the letters, but can't put them in order." This type of introductory work that we do with the older students is very effective in preparing them for working with the first and second graders. They begin the buddy reading experience with some knowledge of what they might find when working with younger learners. They also have a small repertoire of tutoring strategies that they can draw upon. However, we will almost certainly have to return to similar issues throughout the year. As they become more experienced tutors, the students are able to recognize both the accomplishments of their buddies as well as problems grounded in their lack of knowledge of the developmental nature of reading and writing.

**Strategies for tutors who are beginning speakers of English.** An important issue that we have had to attend to relates to the older students in Gail's class who are just beginning to acquire English. As we want to include all the students in the buddy reading experience, a number one priority for us when matching up these particular students is to place them with younger children who share the same native language, whenever possible. We do this so that they are able to build upon the skills that they have in their native language. We have begun to develop libraries of books in Spanish as this is the language spoken by all of the older students in Gail's class who are least fluent in English. We encourage students to read in their native language, but they have the freedom to choose whichever books they wish. We also encourage the students to use either their native language or English when interacting with each other so that they are able to have more in-depth discussions.

There are cases when children do not share a common language, e.g., an older Spanish-speaking student with a younger Laotian-speaking buddy. In these situations, we support the nonfluent English speaking older students in the following ways as they prepare to be tutors:

1. Very limited speakers of English meet in a group with an adult volunteer three times a week for thirty minutes. At these times they read big books in English as these are the books that Mary's class is most familiar with and their predictable elements make them easier for the older students to read. After hearing the volunteer read a book several times so that they are quite familiar with it and understand what it is about, the students practice reading the book to each other—in this way they develop a repertoire of familiar books that they are comfortable reading aloud. So that there are sufficient copies of popular books available, Mary has multiple copies on hand. The students read both fiction and nonfiction big books so that their language and conceptual development are further enhanced.

2. A fluent English-speaking fifth/sixth grader reads a simple book in English to the nonfluent English-speaking classmate. After discussing the book, the nonfluent English speaker practices reading aloud. The day before buddy reading, the nonfluent English speaker selects a book and practices reading it to a peer. Recently, Daniel chose *In a Dark, Dark Wood* (Melser and Cowley 1980). After reading it, he said, "It easy. Next time I want read hard book." He then chose *The Poor Sore Paw* (Cowley 1987f), which contains many more words on a page than *In a Dark, Dark Wood*. After reading it to a peer several times, he was able to read it aloud quite fluently. This practice seemed to give him confidence for the buddy reading session.

3. Books-on-tape are available for the fifth and sixth graders to listen to as often as they wish. We use both commercially produced tapes and recordings of stories that we have made ourselves. We have found that it is helpful to tape stories that have a clearly defined break at the end of each page so that we can use signals to indicate the need to turn pages. This is particularly important for emerging readers. A bell ringing in the middle of the sentence can be very distracting! For signalling page breaks, we have successfully used bells, xylophones, keys, and clickers. When we hear students, colleagues, volunteers, or student teachers do a particularly good job with a read-aloud, we invite them to record the story. The students often have favorite storytellers (frequently people they know), and they will often come back to hear the same stories. We put the tapes and books in large ziplock bags and store them in large bins. The nonfluent speakers of English take the books, tapes, and tape recorders home to listen to the stories and practice them with their family members.

We have learned the importance of spending time preparing the older students before they begin to work with their buddies. Each classroom will have its own particular issues to address, and what we have discussed in the preceding pages reflect the makeup and needs of our students, many of whom are nonnative English speakers.

## Preparing the Younger Students for Buddy Reading

When we first began our buddy reading program six years ago, it didn't occur to us to spend much time with the younger children, other than to remind them of the importance of listening attentively. We now know that it is essential to spend time with the first/second graders if a successful buddy reading experience is to occur. At the beginning of the year, Mary concentrates on a few basic issues with her class such as the purpose of buddy reading, attentive listening, how to respond to books, how to select books, how to read a book, and the respective roles of each buddy.

**Purpose of the buddy reading program.** Each day during the reading block, the first twenty minutes are devoted to sustained reading when children read alone or to each other from self-selected books. This is a time when the children also read aloud to Mary. On many days there is a long line of children arguing with each other about whose turn it is to read to Mary. Mary uses this situation to explain to the children why they will have a buddy to read and write with. The children are invariably very excited about the prospect of having their own partner who will give them their undivided attention.

**Attentive listening strategies.** It is very disconcerting to a person who is reading aloud if the audience is not paying attention, or appears not to be paying attention. We have sometimes noticed that the younger children will engage in quite distracting behaviors that unnerve the older buddies, e.g., looking away, playing with a shoe, sleeve, or pencil, looking at friends, talking with friends, writing on the bottom of their shoes, playing with the velcro on their shoes, and pressing lights on the heels of their shoes.

One day, Katharine was observing sixth grader Manuel reading to first grader Darron. Manuel was not a fluent speaker of English and did not read smoothly or fluently. He would stumble over words, pause in the middle of sentences where the story didn't suggest a pause, and frequently self-correct. Darron had just begun to really break the sound/symbol code and was almost obsessive about the need to read exactly what was on the page. He repeatedly challenged Manuel's reading of the text: "That's not what it says. You gotta read it right!" At one point he said, "You don't read good." At times he would sigh loudly as if impatient with Manuel and look away with a look of derision on his face. We were concerned about this pair, so we observed them closely for a couple of weeks, talked with Manuel (who didn't appear to be rattled by the experience), and realized that we needed to teach the younger children appropriate behaviors for buddy reading.

Mary has relied heavily on role plays to demonstrate successful buddy reading interactional strategies. Usually Mary sets the scene with a brief, focused discussion on the topic, followed by a role play. Recently, her class explored the importance of being an attentive listener:

MARY: Who can tell us what attentive listening is?
MANO: It's when we look at the person who's talking.
MARY: How do we show attentive listening?

KEOVONG: Sit quietly and look at the teacher.

MARY: Just the teacher?

MEL: Look at anyone who's talking.

MARY: I need someone to help show attentive listening. OK, Khanh, come up and help me. I'll be the younger student and you be my older buddy who's reading to me.

Khanh came up and sat in the chair next to Mary. She began to read from a classroom favorite, *The Three Billy Goats Gruff*. "Once upon a time there were three Billy Goats . . ." Mary started to fidget. She looked at the bottom of her shoe. She took a pencil and wrote on the bottom of her shoe, then dropped the pencil and bent under the chair to look for it. Khanh continued reading, glancing at Mary from time to time. The rest of the class giggled and laughed out loud when Mary's behavior was particularly distracting. After Khanh had read a few pages, Mary changed characters and became the teacher again:

MARY: OK, Khanh, you can stop reading now. Was I an attentive listener?

STUDENTS: NOoo! You were bad!

MARILYN: You were playin' with your foot!

YIEN FOU: You was under your chair!

KEOVONG: Not lookin' at your buddy!

MANO: You put her down.

MARY: Khanh, how did I make you feel?

KHANH: Bad, 'Cuz you weren't listenin' to me.

MARY: Alright boys and girls, I was acting very rude! Who can come up and do a better job?

The children clamored to role play and Mary selected Danny to play the part of the older buddy as he is a fairly fluent reader, and Darron to be himself. Darron held the book and looked at it while Danny read. He listened quietly and didn't correct Danny when he stumbled over words. In short, he was much more respectful of and attentive to Danny than he had been with Manuel. After this brief role play, the whole class reviewed what Darron did to show that he was a respectful listener. They generated a list of attentive listening strategies, which the class refers to as their Good Buddy Chart:

1. Sit next to your buddy.
2. Hold the book with your buddy.
3. Listen quietly while your buddy reads.
4. Look at the book when your buddy is reading.
5. Only say good things to your buddy (be polite).

**Responding to books.** One of the most discouraging responses for a person who is reading aloud is to get very little or no response from the audience. Mary therefore spends time talking about the importance of responding to the book or magazine being read aloud. The class talks about several issues, including the following: the importance of asking questions, laughing where appropriate, making comments about the text, making connections between the book and their own experiences and between books, and talking about favorite pictures. She also shows the children how the response does not have to be verbal, that laughing or pointing one's finger at a scene that captures our attention can be a successful way of demonstrating that we are engaged.

Soon after introducing the first and second graders to buddy reading, Mary raises the issue of the younger students taking some responsibility for the discussion. She recently introduced this topic through a very brief minilesson/skit in which second grader Peggy read to Mary from a predictable book, *The Gingerbread Boy* (Galdone 1975). Before beginning the minilesson, Mary had prompted Peggy to ask her at the end of the read-aloud if she had liked the book and what her favorite part was, which she did. Mary simply shrugged her shoulders in response to both questions. The class then talked about how effective Mary's response had been:

MARY: How did I respond to Peggy's questions?
SOU CHING: You did this [he shrugs his shoulders].
DANIELLE: You didn't say nothin'.
MEL: You need to talk.
MARY: Well, what could I have said?
MANO: You could say you like the book.
LIM: I like the book 'cuz it fun. You know when, you know the fox say "Get on my nose."
MALCOLM: I like the words, "Run, run as fast as you can, you can't catch me I'm the Gingerbread Man." [saying it in a sing-song voice].
MARY: Alright. OK. Now, what do we need to remember when we're with our buddies?
MARILYN: You need to talk about the book.
MANO: Tell your favorite part.
DARRON: Show your favorite picture.
MARY: What shall we write on our Good Buddy Chart?
MEL: Talk about the book with your buddy.

Mary wrote "Talk about the book with your buddy" as number six on the class Good Buddy Chart.

**Selecting books.** When the children meet with their older buddies, they take two books with them, one that they can read aloud, and one that they would like their buddy to read to them. On several occasions, children have returned from buddy reading commenting that a book was boring, too long, or not fun to read. In the past, we also noticed that most children randomly selected their books, and we realized that it was important to introduce the children to book selection strategies. Allowing sufficient time for the children to make careful, thoughtful choices is also critical, and Mary allocates at least twenty minutes each week for the whole class to select books (see Photo 5). Throughout the week, of course, the students are continually selecting books, but this is a focused occasion when all the students are engaged in applying what they know about book selection. The children often mention that interesting pictures, a topic that is of interest to them (e.g., animals), and genre (e.g., easy-to-read books, wordless picture books, big books) are key criteria when selecting books.

We show them through role play and discussion how important it is to select books that are interesting to them and likely to be successful choices. In a recent minilesson on book selection, Mary placed on the chalkledge four books that the children were familiar with and that she had read during story time. She did a think aloud in which she explored the process she went through in deciding which two books she was going to take to buddy reading:

PHOTO 5    *Younger students selecting books.*

Let's see, which books do I want to take to buddy reading? I like *The Carrot Seed* (Krauss 1945) because I can read all of it. I also like *The Little Red Hen* (Galdone 1973). I can't read all of it, but I can tell the whole story. I think I'll take *The Little Red Hen* because it's one of my favorite stories. Now, I need to find a second book. The teacher read us *The Elephant and the Bad Baby* (Vipont and Briggs 1986) and it was so funny! I really like this book, but I need someone else to read it to me. I think I'll take this one, too. My buddy can read it to me and she may like it, too.

After this brief role play, Mary asked her students to analyze the strategies she used when selecting her books:

MARY: How did I decide which books I was going to take to buddy reading? Did I grab any two books? What did I do?
MANO: You pick what you like.
KEOVONG: You pick *The Little Red Hen.*
MARY: Why did I pick *The Little Red Hen,* Keovong?
KEOVONG: 'Cuz you like it and you can say it all.
JARVIS: You pick *The Elephant and the Bad Baby* 'cuz you think it funny.
MARY: Can I read this book?
DIEN: No, but your buddy will.
MARY: Alright, boys and girls. Tomorrow we'll be picking two books to take to buddy reading. Remember what you learned today about picking your books.

When the children selected books on the following day, they drew upon what they learned from this minilesson. Keovong came running up to Mary with three books in his arms and said, "Look, look, I can read these two to my buddy. My buddy's gonna' read this to me."

In order to help the students have more success when selecting books, Mary asks them to choose a book and then explain to the class why they selected it (see Photo 6). At the end of the twenty-minute selection time, the children gather on the rug and a few children briefly explain why they selected their books, as the following excerpt illustrates:

MALCOLM: I pick *Frogs* and *Huggles' Breakfast* (Cowley 1987b) 'cuz I can read 'em. I pick this dinosaur book 'cuz I like dinosaurs and I want my buddy to read it to me.
MANO: I like Dr. Seuss and I want my buddy to read to me. I got this book at home.
JARVIS: I got this one [*Lazy Mary* (Melser 1987c), a big book version]. It make me laugh.
MARY: Who's going to read that, you or your buddy?

PHOTO 6    *Younger students explaining their book selection.*

JARVIS: I want my buddy to read it.
MARY: How about you? What do you want to read?
JARVIS: *Yuck Soup* (Cowley 1987g). I know all the words.
SAN CHING: I got that too. We read it yesterday. It easy.
MARY: How about you, Peggy?
PEGGY: I took *Hansel and Gretel* (Gross 1988). You read it to us yesterday and I like when Gretel push the witch in the oven.

In addition to bringing book selection strategies to a conscious level, this kind of regular sharing is also excellent practice for discussing books with their buddies. Mary tries to make this an ongoing part of her reading program. Very often she has another adult in the room and then she divides the students into two groups so that the children get to talk about books more often.

**Reading a book together.**  The younger children like to read to their buddies and we encourage them to do this. However, we have noticed that the children often read with the books right in front of their faces, which has the effect of distancing them from their buddies. We have found it necessary to teach them some shared reading strategies, such as the importance of holding books so that both buddies can see the words and pictures (see Photo 7). A particularly effective strategy is for both children to hold the book at opposite corners. This seems to keep both children's attention.

PHOTO 7   *Reading as a team.*

Most of Mary's students are beginning to recognize that there are
words on the page and they are beginning to use this knowledge when
reading. In these instances, Mary shows the children how to track with
their fingers in order to reinforce their multiple learning modalities
and how words are separated from each other on the page. We do not
introduce this concept as a means to ensure word for word accuracy.
Instead, we introduce it as an emerging reading strategy, a means to
encourage the children to make connections between how words look
on the page (separated from each other) and what we say when
reading aloud. It also helps to reinforce the notion of left-to-right
tracking. Once students are reading fluently, Mary does not encourage this strategy because, when they read larger chunks of text, focusing on individual words will slow them down. When the children
are reading a big book version of a favorite book, they will often use
a pointer for tracking purposes. Although it isn't necessary for the
children to use these pointers when reading one-on-one, the students
often choose to use them. Favorite and inexpensive pointers include
rulers, chopsticks with glitter tips, back scratchers with plastic dinosaur heads, and magician wands.

Many of the children cannot yet read independently, so Mary
spends time showing them how they can still read, e.g., by using the
pictures to tell a story. With more fluent readers, she teaches them
how to use pictures to help predict what will come next. The
younger children usually select a familiar book to read to their

buddy. However, they will sometimes choose an unfamiliar book; for these occasions, Mary shows them how helpful it is to first go through the book from beginning to end to familiarize themselves with the pictures before telling the story. Many of the books that the children select are very familiar to them so that even though they may not be able to read all the words, they have a pretty good sense of the story. Mary urges them to use their knowledge of the story (memory) when reading/telling the story to their buddy.

**Understanding the role of both younger and older buddies.** As we have noticed in past years that the buddy reading sessions can sometimes degenerate into a bit of a battle between the older students and younger children who are testing their buddies, we have found it important to explain the respective roles of the tutors and tutees. Mary spends time discussing with the children the importance of being polite, respectful, and attentive. She explains that their role is to read, listen to books being read to them, and be prepared to talk about the book. She shows them how frustrating it is for the older students when the younger children do not respond; she points out that the older buddies are really interested in what they think and that there aren't any right or wrong answers.

When we first realized that we needed to offer fairly intensive preparation for the students if an effective buddy reading program were to evolve, we focused almost exclusively on the older students, the tutors. More recently, however, we have discovered how important it is to also prepare the younger students. The issues that we have discussed in the preceding pages reflect the particular makeup and needs of Mary's class. Other classes are likely to generate different issues that need to be addressed.

## PAIRING UP CHILDREN

Children need to become familiar with the people with whom they are working so that they feel comfortable and will take risks as readers and writers. We spend time at the beginning of the program discussing the children so that the program is as successful as possible. Many of the children can be randomly paired, but there are several children whom we need to think about very carefully when pairing. For example, Fernando is a very active child who requires a lot of patience on the part of his buddy. We realized that personality, maturity, and interactive skills were very important factors in choosing a buddy for him. We therefore paired Fernando with Vanessa because she is assertive and seems to have a natural talent for working with younger children (e.g., she doesn't get upset when they have a tantrum or refuse to work). In other cases, the reading ability of the children or their fluency in English are the most critical factors.

We establish pairs that may last for the whole year. We have found that the student dyads need to remain constant, at least for several months, so that the children can get to know each other. When pairing up children, we take into consideration a variety of factors, some of which we describe in greater detail in the following pages. However, we should point out that we do not follow any hard and fast rules when pairing children. Instead, the pairing process is very individualized. Some factors that we consider include the following:

1. *Native language.* In the case of children acquiring English as a nonnative language, we take into consideration how fluent they are in English and what their native language is. We have found that this is a particularly critical issue with the older buddies. For example, when matching fifth grader María, who is still relatively new to English and most dominant in Spanish, we paired her with a Spanish-speaking buddy so that they had the option of reading and talking in Spanish. In this way, María was able to more effectively draw upon her extensive knowledge of books.

2. *Reading fluency and experience.* We have found that the degree to which the older buddies are successful readers is a critical issue that we cannot ignore when pairing students. In general, we pair the first/second graders who are not reading independently with strong older readers so that the older buddies are able to help the younger children become better readers. In the past, when we paired fifth/sixth graders who were less fluent readers with first/second graders who were beginning readers, we encountered lots of problems. For example, Richard, a sixth grader, had to focus so hard on his own reading that he was unable to pay attention to the needs of Sammy. The sessions would often disintegrate into Richard reading to himself and Sammy paying more attention to Amphaivane and Sung who were reading across the table from him. We realized that we were expecting too much from the older, struggling readers. Later, after we had assessed the situation, we adjusted some of the pairs and Richard began to work with Monica, a quite fluent and confident first grader. Richard had a more successful experience with Monica as she was able to be a more active and independent reader.

3. *Personality.* This is a fairly subjective factor, but it has proven to be an important one. We look carefully at personalities and try to establish good matches. For example, experience tells us that a shy, quiet older buddy will probably work best with a younger child with a similar personality. We have also learned that matching some of the less self-disciplined younger children with assertive, firm, and nurturing older buddies tends to work out well.

4. *Ethnicity.* Hawthorne draws children from many different cultural and linguistic backgrounds. However, many of our students don't

have opportunities to interact with people from other cultures outside of the school environment and some of the children come with
preconceived stereotypes about other cultures. We have found that
buddy reading is an excellent opportunity for students to get to know
others from a different background, and we try to mix cultures when
pairing students. One of these cross-cultural matchings was between
Malcolm, an African American first grader, and Jesús, a Latino sixth
grader. During the buddy reading sessions, we would often see Jesús
with his arm affectionately wrapped around Malcolm's shoulder and
hear him saying excitedly, "Give me five, Malcolm! You read the
whole book by yourself!" Malcolm's smile, stretching from ear to ear,
indicated how proud he was of himself. We also matched Keovong,
a Laotian first grader, and Juan, a Latino sixth grader. While the
children were making gingerbread houses, Juan was very attentive to
Keovong's needs and patiently instructed him on the construction of
his gingerbread house: "Look Keovong, I brought gum drops and
gummy bears for you. Where do you want to put 'em?" These examples are only two of the many positive cross-cultural interactions
we witness each week during buddy reading. We are hoping that as
the children get older they will remember the positive experiences
they had with their buddies from different cultures.

5. *Attendance.* It is difficult for students to be placed with buddies who
miss a lot of school because they are often left without a partner.
We therefore pair a student who is frequently absent with a pair of
buddies, thus creating a triad. Creating triads is sometimes necessary, anyway, as Gail and Mary rarely have the same number of children. Two younger students may be matched with one older buddy.
On occasion, two older students are placed with a younger buddy.

6. *Children's requests.* For the past few years, Gail and Mary have taught
multi-age classes. Because of this, both teachers have been able to
work with many of the children for two years. We believe that an
important factor in enhancing the buddy reading experience is for
the children to form close relationships with each other. Reflections
written in their journals indicated that many of the children needed
to get to know their buddies well in order to have a successful experience. For example, Soheila wrote the following advice for another
teacher considering starting a buddy reading program: "Have your
kids get to know their buddies first." Jesús wrote, "It's important to
be friendship with them." Therefore, when children make a special
request, e.g., asking to continue working with a buddy from the
previous year, we try to honor that request.

7. *Behavior.* We look at several factors, including degree of self-control,
ability to listen attentively, presence of frequent put-downs, hitting,
biting, teasing, and difficulty staying on task. Every year, a few of the
younger children exhibit these types of behaviors and we carefully

match them with buddies who show maturity and the ability to work easily with younger children.

Matching the children is a complex process. Each of the factors just discussed carries its own weight according to the individual child. For example, whereas fluency in English may be a major factor when pairing a very shy fifth grader who does not have a lot of self-confidence, it may be less of a factor with a risk-taking, self-confident older student. We are constantly in the process of assessing the relative success of the pairs, and on those occasions when there have been sustained problems, we have made changes. Generally speaking, the children will let us know if there's a problem.

We look at challenging children first and figure out good matches for them. For example, Richard is a sixth grade, struggling reader who lacks confidence. When reading with adults, he has exploded in anger when confronted by text that he has not been able to read. We are concerned that he have a successful buddy reading experience. We also realize that some of the strategies that he is being taught for working with younger children (e.g., focusing on meaning rather than decoding accuracy, utilizing the pictures to help with word decoding, and reading familiar books repeatedly) are strategies that can help him as a reader. By exposing him to them in this context, we have found that he is more willing to read texts that are more accessible to him and therefore gets practice using reading strategies that can be helpful to him. Because of these issues, we placed him with Sammy, a happy-go-lucky first grader who was not yet reading and would probably not challenge Richard's own emerging reading. Later in the semester, however, we saw that Richard was having a hard time keeping Sammy's attention as he, Richard, struggled so hard to make meaning, in the consequence seeming to forget that he was reading to Sammy. He would begin by holding the book so that both he and Sammy could see the pages of the book, but ultimately, as Richard concentrated on reading, the book came closer to him, and Sammy would have to peer over the top of the book in order to see; eventually Sammy would lose interest and direct his attention elsewhere.

As Richard had also been absent quite a bit and we thought that Sammy needed to be engaged more in order to become a reader, we decided it might be better if Richard were placed with another, less distractable child, and Sammy with an older student who had demonstrated the ability to handle more difficult children . . . and wasn't also a struggling reader. We made this change about midway through the semester. Sammy began to work with Angelina. Richard started to work with Monica. These changes worked out well. Angelina was much firmer with Sammy, which led to him becoming more attentive and a more focused reader. Monica is a much stronger reader than

Sammy and she would read to Richard, who would listen and follow along in the text. We had not anticipated the way in which this pair would work out so well—the chemistry between them was extraordinary—and we are still not sure what caused its success.

If a dyad is not working out, the teachers need to discuss the problem with the children and, if there is no workable solution, offer an alternative pairing. For example, José brought up difficulties he was having with Lim on several occasions. He talked about how Lim showed no respect for him: he would swear, get up and meander around the room, walk to the water fountain and get drinks, visit his friends, or look at books in the library. The class discussed his dilemma and offered several suggestions (e.g., pick a shorter book, find out what kind of books he likes, tell Ms. Pippitt), none of which had worked for José. After four weeks of José trying to work out the problem, and us observing them working together, we decided to separate them. Once Lim began to work with Phath, Lim stopped his rude behavior. José was delighted with his new partner, Astrid.

Another problematic situation that we had to deal with involved José Luis and his younger buddy, Josie, who was clearly unhappy during buddy reading. From the minute she came into the upper grade classroom, she cried. And cried. And cried relentlessly. Mary wondered if Josie's tears were due to sickness as José Luis did not appear to be doing anything to upset her. In fact, he is a soft-spoken, attentive young person who is not prone to behavior that might upset a younger child. José Luis was beside himself and didn't know what to do, and we were concerned that this experience would undermine his self-esteem. When we could not figure out the origins of Josie's distress, we decided to keep her in Mary's classroom, which involved changing partners. To our relief, Josie was relaxed with her new partner, and both she and José Luis had a successful year with their new partners. Later, we wondered if going into the fifth/sixth-grade classroom had made Josie feel insecure.

On occasion, we have had to attend to difficulties that are grounded in the older buddy's inexperience with buddy reading and lack of knowledge about the developmental nature of emergent language and literacy. One example of this type of problem involved Peter, a newcomer to Gail's class. He was paired with Marilyn for his first buddy reading session and, in the debriefing session that followed, he raised a concern:

PETER: Yes, there's a problem. My buddy doesn't know how to spell. Words like *hippopotamus*.
GAIL: Uh huh. So, what did you do?
PETER: I had her write each word she got wrong five times.
SEVERAL STUDENTS: What?! You did what?

VILIPHONE: That's a put-down! That's a punishment!
DAMLONGSONG: That's like writing lines.

Initially, Gail felt extremely proud of her students' responses. It was clear to her that they understood inappropriate ways to address writing miscues, and she was thrilled. She was also delighted that they could spot the limitations in something that was commonplace and had been ingrained in them from their own early school experiences (how unhelpful it is to spell incorrectly spelled words over and over again). She hadn't realized until then that they were aware of the limitations and punitive nature of such a teaching strategy. She also realized that the minilessons were paying off, which was reassuring.

At the same time, however, Gail saw how crestfallen Peter looked and realized that he had been doing his best with limited resources at hand as this was the first time that he had been a part of buddy reading. After all, she thought, he was almost certainly drawing upon the strategies that he had been exposed to as a student. She was concerned that Peter was feeling attacked and interrupted the students, reminding them that Peter was new to the class and was just learning how to be a tutor. She commented that she had seen how hard he had worked with Marilyn, and that he thought that he had asked Marilyn to do the right thing. The class then talked about experiences they had had as learners that were similar. In the process, they seemed to become more understanding of Peter's actions. Gail took this opportunity to remind the whole class that the younger students were just learning to read and write and needed a lot of support. The class then discussed ways in which they could deal with similar situations, and their suggestions included, "Don't say anything," and "Let them spell it the way they want."

It's always gratifying to be able to report that problematic situations have been resolved beautifully, but that isn't how life is in many situations. This is true for Peter. He remained at the school for only five or six more weeks, and during that time he never enjoyed buddy reading sessions. "I hate this" or "This is dumb," he would say to Gail and anyone else who would listen as the class got ready for the sessions. Gail wishes that she had made time to talk with him about these feelings. We suspect that he was discouraged by his peers' condemnation of his actions on that first day when he raised his problem. This situation also made us realize that fifth- and sixth-grade newcomers should be provided with some orientation to buddy reading and lots of support before being invited to work one-on-one with a younger student. We feel that our lack of attention to this very important detail contributed to Peter's negative attitude towards buddy reading.

Because of absences and children leaving the school, there are often occasions when children do not have a partner. If an older buddy is absent, the younger child is placed with another pair for that meeting. If a younger child is absent, we sometimes ask their buddies to act as observers, keep field notes, and report back to the whole class on their observations at the end of the buddy reading session. Each Tuesday morning, we quickly check on who is absent and make short-term changes to accommodate absent children and relocate children whose partners have moved away from the school. Periodically, we sit down together to assess how well the pairs are working. It was on one of these occasions that we realized that Antoine's buddy had left town and we needed to find a replacement for him. As we went through the two class lists and noted other changes, we realized that we would have to break up a successful partnership if Antoine, a sixth grader, were to have a partner. The problem that then loomed was that Antoine had not been a very effective buddy. He was usually more interested in what other pairs of students were doing, would talk with his friends, and often got into altercations with his peers. We considered asking Antoine to join another pair, but realized that that wouldn't work out because he had trouble concentrating in the presence of his peers. It then dawned on us that we had been talking earlier about the need to ask the older children to periodically observe each other in order to better understand and learn from the buddy reading process. Antoine became an observer and kept field notes on various pairs. During the debriefing session following buddy reading, Antoine shared his observations with the class. While these are some strategies that we have tried when students are absent, we are continually searching for other roles for students who are unexpectedly left without a partner.

This attention in the beginning of the year to carefully pairing the buddies is crucial to ensuring the success of the program. However, even with the most careful selection, problems are likely to occur while the relationships are developing. We do not think that it is a good idea to respond to conflicts by immediately changing the pairs, even though the students may request a new buddy. When this occurs, we make a point of observing the pairs to assess the situation and in preparation for conferring with the students and with each other. Most of the time, these conflicts are resolved through debriefing sessions, minilessons in both classes, or individual conferences.

## STRATEGIES FOR GETTING TO KNOW EACH OTHER

We have found that it is critical that the pairs of children have a chance to get to know each other before they ever share books together as this seems to be a key ingredient in successful buddy reading relationships. Esmeralda captured this sentiment in the following written reflection:

> What I've learned from buddy reading is that you have to be
> friends with them to teach them how to read because if you're not
> friends with your buddy they are going to be afraid of reading to
> you because if they make a mistake they are going to think that you
> are going to be mad at them, so you've got to learn to be nice to
> you're buddy and be friends with you're buddy.

We have had a lot of success with "inclusion" activities from a community building program, "Tribes" (Gibbs 1994). This program is
intended to improve students' academic achievement and self-
esteem by creating a safe and supportive environment, one in which
all members of the classroom community respect differences and are
willing to take risks. Class members are encouraged to express their
feelings, share their cultural traditions and values, and learn to be
attentive and respectful listeners. By creating a warm and supportive
atmosphere, the chances of the reading and writing tutoring experience succeeding are enhanced.

On the first day of buddy reading this year, we explained to the
two classes that they would meet their buddy through a simple
puzzle-matching game. The teachers explained that they were to
find their partner by matching their puzzle piece, figure out which
classroom they would be working in (the teacher's initial on the
back of the puzzle indicated this), and meet in that classroom. On
one puzzle piece was the name of the younger buddy. The older
buddy's name was on the other piece (see Figure 7). The two classes
met in the patio separating the two classrooms. For the next few
minutes the children moved amongst each other excitedly looking
for the match to their puzzle. "Oh, I got Manop!" yelled Lance.
"Mano's mine," shouted Choulaphone as she put her arm around
her buddy and hugged her close to her. An enormous smile envel-
oped her face. Holding hands, the buddy pairs began to move into
the two classrooms and when we entered the classrooms, we found
that the pairs of students were already totally engrossed in reading
books together. The follow-up inclusion activity that we had planned
was obviously not needed as the children were absorbed and comfortable with each other.

We have also used other inclusion activities successfully. We hope
that teachers find the following suggestions helpful:

8. *Interviews.* Students learn about each other through interviews that
   focus on favorite hobbies, TV shows, or food; native language; and
   place of birth. After spending about ten minutes interviewing their
   buddies, all the students sit in a large circle and take turns introducing their buddies to the rest of the class.
9. *People hunts.* As in a scavenger hunt, pairs of students have a list of
   questions for which they have to find answers from within the class

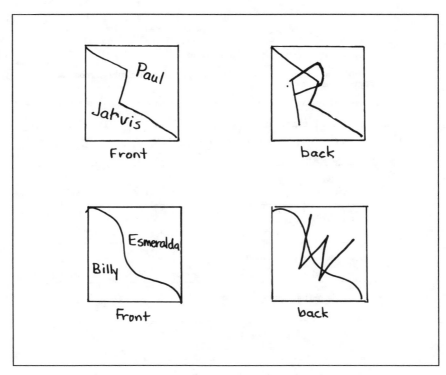

FIGURE 7   *Name puzzle: A matching game.*

(e.g., find a person who has two brothers, has a cat at home, was born the same month as the younger buddy). The older buddy's role is to help the younger buddy understand the questions and facilitate finding the answers. See Figure 8 for an example of a people hunt sheet that we have used.

10. *Interactive or cooperative games and activities.* In cooperative games, the older students read the directions while the younger students look for the appropriate items. For example, in a shape and color hunt, pairs of students go outside and find things on the yard with a specific shape and color, for instance something brown that is triangular in shape. Cooking and craft activities that require collaboration, e.g., making gingerbread houses (where one person needs to hold the walls while the other glues them together), have also worked well with our students. These activities allow the students to get to know each other in a relaxed, but focused way. We have found that social occasions (eating lunch together or having a pizza party) often do not work out well as the older students want to socialize with their own classmates. Activities such as those described above seem to work better.

Once the students have received some preparation for buddy reading, and have had an opportunity to get to know each other,

---

**A People Hunt**

With your buddy, find a person for each item. The younger buddy will ask the questions and the older buddy will write the names on the line.

1. Find a person who was born the same month as the younger buddy:

_____

2. Find a person who was born the same month as the older buddy:

_____

3. Find a person who has a dog at home:

_____

4. Find a person who likes to draw:

_____

5. Find a person who has more than two sisters:

_____

6. Find a person who can roll their tongue:

_____

7. Find a person who can speak two languages:

_____

8. Find a person who was born outside the United States:

_____

9. Find a person who was born in the United States:

_____

10. Find a person who is a conflict manager:

_____

---

FIGURE 8    *A people hunt.*

they are ready to embark on the aspect of the experience that they usually enjoy the most—working together on a weekly basis.

## BEGINNING THE BUDDY READING PROGRAM

We have initiated buddy reading exchanges without any preparation, and it is very tempting to do so, particularly when one is excited after first hearing about it, but we have learned to proceed more cautiously. As can be seen, we put in a lot of time and effort preparing students for buddy reading. Although they are anxious to begin right away, we have learned that it's worthwhile to initially focus on preparing them so that they have a more successful experience right from the beginning. After the month-long preparation, the students are ready to meet and work with each other. Once this happens, however, our work as observers and teachers does not end. Instead, we move into a phase of teaching that involves careful observing, listening, and tailoring instruction and support to the needs of the students. The preparation that we have described in this chapter helps a great deal in ensuring a successful buddy reading program, but we have found that ongoing preparation is necessary if a successful program is to be maintained. We will address this issue in the next chapter.

# 3

# "And When I Make It Ixided We Never Have Probems Together."

## Maintaining a Buddy Reading Program

Since taking a more careful look at how much more can be accomplished when students receive ongoing preparation, we have placed considerably more attention on this. We have discovered that the successful maintenance of a buddy reading program depends upon the ongoing preparation of the children. What we see and hear as we move around the room during buddy reading, what we hear in the debriefing sessions that occur at the close of each session, and what we read in their logs guide us as teachers. Preparation occurs in three basic formats: a) focused, whole class instruction each week before the children meet with their buddies (minilessons), usually lasting about ten minutes, b) very brief one-on-one coaching during buddy reading, and c) exploration of student-generated issues in the debriefing sessions held at the end of each buddy reading session. In many cases, the content of the preparation in the two classrooms is often similar, but as the two groups of children have different roles, the depth and focus is usually different. That is why we will explore this element of buddy reading from two perspectives, the older children (the tutors) and the younger children (the tutees).

## ONGOING PREPARATION OF THE OLDER STUDENTS (THE TUTORS)

In some respects, Gail's class is engaged in early teacher preparation. The issues that we have explored with the students are very similar to those we discuss in teacher credential program classes. When we see a common need, we teach the whole class in minilessons. As we circulate around the classroom during buddy reading, we offer support in brief one-on-one conferences—these are times when we take advantage of "teachable moments." The debriefing sessions provide us with invaluable information that influences the content of future minilessons and the organization of the buddy reading program.

## Using Minilessons

At the beginning of the school year, many of the minilessons are devoted to procedural issues, such as when to write in the log and when to draw a picture. However, in the course of the year, many other issues get addressed, as Figure 9 illustrates. We have organized the minilessons in this chart into three categories:

1. *Procedural issues.* This involves what books to pick, schedule of activities, and record keeping.
2. *Beginning reading and writing strategies.* This includes bedtime reading strategies, and skills and strategies that support emergent readers and writers.
3. *Social, interactional, and management issues.* This includes attentive listening, questioning techniques, showing respect, and handling inappropriate behavior.

We should point out that many minilessons often bridge more than one category, although we always limit our focus to a dominant theme so that their content is accessible to the students. For example, a minilesson that focused on ways to talk about books (in the "beginning reading and writing strategies" category) also touched on the importance of not using judgmental language with the younger students (in the "interactional issues" category). Although we use a variety of strategies for sharing teaching and interactional approaches, we have found role playing to be a particularly effective strategy (see Photo 8). In the following pages, we describe six minilessons that illustrate the process through which we go when exploring issues in this way.

**Encouraging the younger buddies to read and write on their own.**
In preparation for one day's buddy reading session, Mary asked Gail to remind the older students that the first and second graders should be doing some reading and writing on their own during buddy reading. Mary had noticed that many of the older children were doing everything for their buddies, albeit in a well-meaning way. Several of the younger children were unhappy that they did not have a more active role, and, in a debriefing session, said that they wanted to read and write themselves. Sounthavy said, "My buddy won't let me write. He write it all for me. I already know how to write." "Me too, " added Peggy. "I can write some words, too, and she (her buddy) all the time

**PROCEDURAL ISSUES:**
*RECORD KEEPING*
How to record books
> Keeping field notes

*ORDER OF ACTIVITIES*
When to read
> When to write in logs
> When to draw in logs
> Appropriate time to begin projects

*CHOOSING BOOKS*
Awareness of buddy's interest
> Familiarity with a large variety of titles and authors of children's literature
> Awareness of personal favorites (titles and authors)
> Where to find books

**BEGINNING READING AND WRITING STRATEGIES**
*BEDTIME READING STRATEGIES*
How to sit
> Reading with expression
> How to hold a book

*SUPPORTING EMERGING READERS*
Accepting what buddies volunteer
> Using pictures to tell stories
> Importance of rereading favorite books
> Taking turns reading
> Echo reading
> Tracking when reading
> Stages of emergent reading

*READING STRATEGIES*
How to read non-fiction
> How to handle inappropriate or difficult books
> Role of prediction when reading
> Questioning strategies in discussions

*WRITING STRATEGIES*
Taking dictation
> Using invented spelling
> Printing vs. cursive
> Beginning consonants
> Role of drawing in early writing
> Stages of early writing

**SOCIAL, INTERACTIONAL, AND MANAGEMENT ISSUES**
*INTERACTIONAL SKILLS*
Responding to buddy's talk—following the lead of the buddy
> Asking open-ended questions
> Encouraging younger students to read and write for themselves
> Sharing own responses to books
> Having a discussion after reading a book

*MANAGEMENT*
How to handle bad language
> How to handle inattentiveness
> How to work with two students
> Alternatives to bribes and treats
> Time allocations—managing time between reading and writing

*SOCIAL SKILLS*
Attentive listening
> Showing respect for buddy

FIGURE 9 *List of minilessons taught to the fifth and sixth graders.*

Photo 8    *Role play during a minilesson.*

write for me.'' Mary later gave this feedback to Gail, who passed on the message to her own class in a minilesson:

> Ms. Pippitt really wants her students to read so they can practice their reading. We want you to have your buddy read to you first before you read to them. She also wants her students to begin to write each week. So she's giving them a special notebook. Their literature log. When you're finished reading, she would like them to choose their favorite book and write about it in their logs. All right? Ask them what they liked about the book and let them write about it in their logs.

**Taking dictation.** On another occasion, Gail explained how Mary wanted the tutors to assist her in assessing how much knowledge the younger children had gained from a unit on penguins that they were finishing up. Although Mary normally asks her students to write on their own, for this assessment task, she wanted the older children to take dictation for the younger children because writing often interrupted the flow of ideas. The upper-grade class reviewed how they could help their buddies:

GAIL: Now when they write, some of the second graders can write by themselves. If they can't spell a word, what are you going to ask them?

TAMARA: Sound it out.

GAIL: Sound it out? If they say "No," what can you do?

JUAN: Help them.

GAIL: How would you help them, Juan?

JUAN: The first letter and then . . .

GAIL: If it's the word *monster*. Sound it out with them. What would you say, Juan?

JUAN: I don't know. Is it monster? M-o-nnn [Sounding out M-O-N].

GAIL: What questions would you ask them? (You could ask) what sounds do you hear? [pause] If you have a first grader and they say "No, I don't want to write, I can't write," then you could say, "Would you like me to help you?" Remember how Pamela said, "I don't want to write." And what did I do?

TAMARA: Write for her.

GAIL: I wrote for her. So, she told me everything she wanted to say and I wrote it for her. Be sure when you write you don't use cursive, you print for them. Write neatly so they can go back and read your writing. OK? This is one way to help them learn how to read because you're writing their story. They're telling you their story. And you write exactly like they say it. Use the exact words that they're telling you.

This minilesson illustrates how important it is for teachers to work closely together. Gail and Mary agree that young children should be encouraged to write their own messages however they are able. If the two teachers had not coordinated their planning for buddy reading, there could have been confusion as to what the children were expected to do. This type of clarity of directions and consistency of instruction was not always present, and Gail and Mary eventually became aware of the fact that they needed to coordinate their instructions as they sometimes inadvertently gave mixed messages to their students.

**Procedure for writing in logs.** One example of how children seem to have different notions of what they needed to be doing was illustrated when the older students wrote in their logs. Sometimes they would start recording their entries before their younger buddies had finished reading their books. For example, while Keovong was reading a book to his older buddy, Juan, the older boy was busy writing the title, author, genre, and theme of the book in his reading log. We realized that Juan was showing considerably more interest in the mechanics of recording the entry than in listening to Keovong read. We wondered whether we had inadvertently contributed to the problem as we had emphasized to all the students that they needed to keep a record of their reading for future reference (e.g., in order to make recommendations to other students). This practice of the older children writing prematurely in their reading logs often distracted the first and second graders and gave the impression that the older students did not value their efforts. It was clear to us that we needed to address this issue with the older children, which we did in a minilesson. As the class discussed the most appropriate timing for reading, writing, and talking, and reasons for engaging in each during buddy reading, Gail wrote notes on the dry erase board:

1. Discuss book.
2. Buddies write in logs.
3. Buddies draw pictures.
4. Write in your own logs.

This minilesson reminded students that their primary purpose in meeting with their younger buddies was to share books, orally interact with each other, and respond to books in writing.

**Ways of responding to nonfiction books and magazines.** At another time, we realized that the older students needed help in exploring ways to read and talk about nonfiction books and magazines. We had observed two older children, TJ and Josh, accompany first grader Jon on a foray into the classroom library to select books to replace the picture books that Jon had indicated he had no interest in reading or listening to. They returned to their table with two issues of the children's nature magazine, *Ranger Rick*. When TJ asked Jon which magazine he wanted to start with, Jon selected the magazine with a frog on the front cover. TJ then told him to sound out *frog*, which was on the front cover. As they turned the pages of the magazine, TJ attempted to read all the words in the text and in captions. From time to time, TJ would insist that Jon sound out words, an almost impossible task for both of them, and after a while, Josh chimed in, "Jon, this book is too old for you. You can't understand." As if remembering that they should be enjoying the reading experience, TJ responded, "We're suppose to be just looking at the pictures," but they continued to focus on sounding out the words. Eventually Josh suggested, "Let's go and pick a good book." After observing and talking about this incident, we realized that we needed to talk with the older students about strategies to use when a text did not lend itself to a traditional read-aloud. In the next week's minilesson, Gail and Soheila, one of the sixth graders, role-played reading a nonfiction text. Gail held up several nonfiction books and magazines and explained, "Many of your buddies choose these books and magazines because they have beautiful animal pictures. However, they are very difficult to read. Watch us and look for strategies that I use to read this magazine with Soheila." As the older students watched and kept notes, Soheila and Gail began the role play:

GAIL: What book do you want to read today, Soheila?

SOHEILA: I brought this magazine about bears. I love bears.

GAIL: Why do you like bears?

SOHEILA: They're my favorite animal. I have a big brown bear in my bedroom.

GAIL: Let's look at the pictures to see what we can learn about bears. [They turn to a picture of a bear catching a fish in a river.]

GAIL: What's happening here?

SOHEILA: The bear has a fish.

GAIL: Oh, yeah. It looks like a salmon.

SOHEILA: What's a salmon?

GAIL: It's a kind of fish that you find in the north where the bears live. Bears love to catch the salmon as they swim up the river.

SOHEILA: Oh, [turning the page] look at that. They're so cute, those babies. You know they're called cubs.

GAIL: Uh huh. Oh, look, there's three of them.

SOHEILA: That one looks just like my stuffed one. I saw one like that at the zoo. Last year we went on a field trip and I saw lots of different bears. One was real big and I even saw a polar bear. They have fur on their feet.

GAIL: It sounds like you really like bears, Soheila, and know a lot about them. Thanks for sharing.

At the end of the role play, the class explored what Gail had done to involve Soheila in reading the magazine and then generated a list of strategies to use when reading nonfiction to the younger students. As the students spoke, Katharine wrote their suggestions on the dry erase board:

1. Just look at the pictures and talk about them.
2. Ask open-ended questions.
3. Skip pages, if you need to.
4. Skip words you don't know.
5. Change words.

**Ways of talking about books.** Several issues are originally explored in the orientation to buddy reading during the first month and are then returned to throughout the year, as the need arises. As the success of the program hinges on sharing books that fascinate and entertain the readers and listeners, we have used minilessons to revisit issues surrounding the selection of good books. Other minilessons explore read-aloud strategies because the way we read to others has a profound impact on the success of the session. Throughout the year, the older students have opportunities to read both new and familiar books to each other so that they can practice read-aloud strategies. In other minilessons, Gail has addressed how to talk about books. These minilessons evolved after we noticed that the older students rarely shared their own reactions to a book. Instead of the vibrant and animated discussions that we had seen these students engage in when talking about books with their peers, we saw discussions that resembled "grand inquisitions" that didn't seem to have any intrinsic purpose other than to bring the book-reading to closure. An example follows:

JOSH: Did you like the book?
PHONESAVANH: Yes.
JOSH: What did you like about it?
PHONESAVANH: I dunno.
JOSH: Who was your favorite character?
PHONESAVANH: The frog.
JOSH: Why?
PHONESAVANH: I dunno.

By asking the students to bring their reactions to a conscious level and explain them, we are offering them opportunities to synthesize their observations and analyze what contributed to their reactions. In this way, they are able to better understand more difficult concepts or texts. For example, when they do not understand the actions of a character, why the setting is described in such detail, or the author's purpose in writing the book, they often ask their peers for clarification. The discussion that follows often enhances their understanding, and proves to be a very effective strategy for gaining understanding. Both the accomplished and less experienced fifth- and sixth-grade readers benefit from discussions that are grounded in shorter and, often, less complex texts. It is like practice for them.

As we have become more skilled observers of children, we have noticed occasional unsupportive behaviors that tended to undermine the buddy reading experience, e.g., older students paying more attention to a peer at a neighboring table, not showing much enthusiasm for the younger children's early efforts at reading and writing, chiding their buddies for reading the wrong word, or being unnecessarily impatient. Although these behaviors do not occur often, we address these issues with individual children who seem to be caught in a pattern of unsupportive behavior, and with the whole class in minilessons, when that is appropriate. We have conducted minilessons on accepting buddy responses to books, the value of rereading favorite books (some of the buddies were chiding their buddies for bringing the same books week after week), taking turns reading, responding to buddy questions and comments, and following up on a buddy's comments.

**Strategies for working with children acquiring English as a nonnative language.** As so many of Mary's students are nonnative English speakers and several are just beginning to acquire English, we have found it important to use minilessons to explore strategies for working with children who are in the process of becoming bilingual. Gail's students have learned about ESOL (English to Speakers of Other Languages) and how to incorporate appropriate strategies into their buddy reading meetings. We have found that the following strategies have worked particularly well for the older students when they are working with younger buddies who are not yet fluent in English:

1. Read books that have been written by the younger students. Children love to read what their peers have written and, as the content is often familiar and the language relatively simple, these books are excellent reading materials and work particularly well with the children acquiring English. The first and second graders write both individual and class books and these, along with those written by previous classes, are available for the children to read during buddy reading.
2. Read books that have been written by the older students. As the fifth and sixth graders write books for the younger children, the collection of student-authored books has grown enormously. Commercially published "controlled readers" that have been written for ESOL students do not generally work as well as these books, because meaning and engagement are often lost at the expense of simplicity of language or grammatical structures.
3. Select books that have only a few words. Many of the books published by The Wright Group and Rigby publishers (usually available in both big book and standard sizes) have worked particularly well. Although the books have only a few words, they explore topics in interesting ways and the pictures help to convey meaning, often in humorous ways. See the Appendix for additional suggestions.
4. Select books with a highly developed predictable pattern. Many of the younger children choose these books because the predictable text is easily learned and there are many contextual clues, thereby contributing to a successful reading experience. Some favorites include *The Very Busy Spider* (Carle 1986), *The Little Red Hen* (Galdone 1973), *The Three Billy Goats Gruff* (Galdone 1981), *Oh, A-Hunting We Will Go* (Langstaff 1974), *Rosie's Walk* (Hutchins 1968), *Twenty-four Robbers* (Wood 1980), and *Brown Bear, Brown Bear* (Martin 1970). See the Appendix for additional suggestions.
5. Select nonfiction books and magazines that focus on a topic that is particularly interesting to the younger buddies. In this way, children acquiring English are able to draw upon their prior knowledge. See the Appendix for suggestions.
6. Read the same book often so that it becomes very familiar. As the older children become more familiar with a text, we notice that their reading becomes more animated and they take on the roles of the different characters. When the older buddies read with expression,

the younger students become more interested in the story and they gain a greater understanding of the book.

7. Point to the pictures and talk about them a lot. This "picture walk" prepares the children for reading the text. If they discuss the pictures prior to reading, they are better prepared to read some of the words. Discussing the pictures also develops interest in the book and involves the children in predicting what is going to happen in the book.

8. Use gestures to explain concepts and clarify points. We noticed that some of the older children would naturally act out certain words, e.g., pointing to the sky and making an arc to demonstrate "rainbow," pumping their arms to act out "jogging," or putting an imaginary spoon to the mouth for "eating."

9. Paraphrase and talk about the pictures as you go along so that the children have many chances to understand the content.

10. Speak clearly and loudly enough for the younger students to hear. On occasion, we would notice that some of the older students were very absorbed in a story and ended up reading in a soft voice, as if to themselves. The younger students would often begin to lose interest.

11. Select texts whose content is either familiar to the children or similar to texts they have read or heard in the native language. Folk and fairy tales that occur in many cultures allow children to bring prior knowledge to the reading experience. For example, there are hundreds of versions of the Cinderella story, and the first and second graders have particularly enjoyed the Chinese version, *Lon Po Po* (Young 1989).

12. Prior to reading the book, talk about it in the native language of the younger learner. If the book is available in a language other than English, read that version first and then read the English version so that students have a better understanding of what the story is about.

We have learned to limit ourselves to one, or, at most, two main points or strategies for each minilesson, and to limit the amount of time we devote to these lessons—ten to fifteen minutes seems to be the optimum amount of time. Although the class frequently raises many issues whenever there is a discussion, we have learned to discipline ourselves and limit the focus of a minilesson. We have found that, on those occasions when we have explored too many topics or let the minilesson go on too long, students begin to lose interest. Through minilessons, we try to make sure that the older students have the information, knowledge, skills, and strategies needed to effectively relate to and work with their buddies.

## Using One-on-One Coaching

As we walk around the room during buddy reading, we are carefully paying attention to what students are doing and saying in their pairs. These observations inform us about students (e.g., about their uses of oral and written language, and their interactional skills and strategies), and guide us in making instructional decisions. Sometimes observations provide us with general information that we decide is appropriate for whole class instruction via a minilesson. At other times, what we observe is highly idiosyncratic and merits individualized attention, as in one-on-one coaching. For example, as we circulate around the room, we might notice a student who is doing a particularly good job of reading aloud or handling an uncooperative buddy, and we will quietly, and as unobtrusively as possible, acknowledge that student's efforts. This happened one day, a week after the fifth and sixth graders had complained that their buddies did not pay enough attention and were not listening to them reading. Gail decided to address the issue through a minilesson devoted to exploring how important it is to read with expression and use different voices to represent different characters. Once the students were working together, we focused our observations on how effectively the older students were reading aloud. Mary was moving around the room, listening in and taking notes, and she stopped for a few minutes to observe Tamara reading *The Three Billy Goats Gruff* (Galdone 1981) to her buddy, Eata. Tamara's voice was deep and emphatic as she read the Troll's words, and when she read the little Billy Goat Gruff's part, her voice was high and squeaky. Eata's eyes were wide open and her mouth registered a huge smile. There was no question that Eata was listening and was engaged. As she passed beside Tamara, Mary whispered, "I really enjoyed listening to you reading. I could see those characters in the voices you used!"

Sometimes our coaching in the form of encouragement can have an unexpected effect. One day, Amphaivane was reading *Cloudy With a Chance of Meatballs* (Barrett 1978) with a great deal of verbal and non-verbal expression. Many of the children sitting at neighboring tables had stopped what they were doing to listen to Amphaivane's rendition of the story. Katharine and Gail were also mesmerized by the dramatic and compelling way she was reading the story. Standing nearby, they glanced and smiled at each other and, in undertones, agreed that she was doing an excellent job with her read-aloud. As Gail and Katharine passed Amphaivane and her partner Sung, Katharine bent down and quietly congratulated Amphaivane on doing such a good job of reading the story with expression. Later, in the debriefing session, Gail commented to the whole class that she had been very impressed with Amphaivane's expressive reading.

Soon after buddy reading began the following week, however, we were startled by the sound of Amphaivane's voice booming across the room as she shouted the entire story to her partner. Unlike the earlier read-aloud, she did not differentiate between sections of the book or characters, and the expression she was putting into her reading seemed unrelated to the words and story. Periodically, she glanced up at us, as if for approval. In contrast to the admiring reception her reading had generated from her peers the previous week, this time her booming voice was so distracting that some children called out to her to be quiet. We wondered whether our private and public congratulations had somehow led to this overuse of dramatic reading strategies, whether our congratulations had the opposite effect of what we intended. Gail whispered to Katharine, "Oh no, have we created a monster?!" Up to this point, our unobtrusive congratulations had not had this kind of effect; instead, they had seemed to act more as support and reinforcement. We knew it would not be appropriate to intervene with Amphaivane at that moment —we sensed that to do so would be very demoralizing and disruptive to her. To be honest, we were puzzled and not sure how to handle it. Later, in the debriefing session, Gail commented on how she had noticed many students reading with lots of expression, which brought the book alive, but that they had to be careful about not overdoing dramatic readings. In retrospect, it probably would have been helpful to talk privately with Amphaivane; by not approaching her directly, we may have missed a very good opportunity of finding out about influences on her read-aloud decisions.

At other times, our coaching focuses on actually teaching a strategy in a very short and focused way. This will usually happen when we have seen a student struggling, perhaps with a teaching or interactional strategy that doesn't appear to be working well. For example, one day Katharine was observing Manuel and his first grade buddy, Darron. They were both writing in their logs, and Darron repeatedly asked Manuel how to spell words, which Manuel tried to do. However, he was becoming a bit frustrated, particularly when he wasn't sure himself how to spell the words. Sometimes he would turn to Katharine for help. She then quietly suggested to Manuel that he invite Darron to listen to words and try to figure out what sounds he could hear. She quickly demonstrated to both boys and then went back to her notetaking, turning her body slightly so that she was observing another pair of students. At first, both Manuel and Darron were hesitant and looked over to Katharine repeatedly, but once they seemed to realize that they were on their own, they got into a pattern of listening carefully to the sounds in words that they were unsure of; in fact, both boys began to use the same strategy while writing.

On another day, when Gail was observing Sammy and Richard, she noticed that the older boy was not aware of how difficult it was for Sammy to see the book that he was reading aloud. After watching this for several minutes and noticing how Sammy was becoming increasingly less interested and more distracted, Gail moved behind Richard and whispered: "I don't think Sammy can see. Why don't you ask him to hold one corner of the book while you hold the other." Richard looked up with a faint look of astonishment on his face, smiled, nodded, lowered the book so that it was propped on the table and invited Sammy to rejoin the read-aloud: "Hey, Sammy, take this here." For the rest of the buddy reading session, Richard and Sammy held the book together, and were obviously sharing more than had been apparent in previous sessions. Gail had intervened because she was afraid that Richard's lack of awareness of Sammy's needs would further exacerbate an already difficult buddy pairing.

In the past, we were reluctant to intervene on the spot, either to congratulate or to make suggestions, because we did not want to do anything that would undermine the students' efforts. Instead, we would wait until the debriefing session to discuss an issue, if that seemed to be the most appropriate time to raise it. Or, if it was not an issue that was of relevance to the whole class, we vowed to talk with the student in question after the buddy reading session. However, we found that many of the issues we had noticed while observing did not come up for discussion in the debriefing sessions. Also, we often ran out of time because lunch followed buddy reading, and we were unable to give pertinent, immediate feedback to individual students. We began to realize that we were losing out on "teachable moments." We were originally very reluctant to intervene; we are still very careful about when and how we interject comments and suggestions.

## Using Debriefing Sessions

After each week's buddy reading session, when the fifth- and sixth-grade students reconvene in their classroom, the first thing they do is reflect in writing upon their experiences (see Photo 9). They do this in preparation for a class discussion that follows the ten- to fifteen-minute quiet time devoted to thinking and writing. By doing this, the students are able to take a step back from the activity, reflect upon what happened, assess its success, and become more conscious of factors that influence learning. The students usually comment on what happened or how things went and why they went the way they did, but their entries reflect the many issues they encounter on any given day. Sometimes they write about their buddies' behaviors and learning processes, as this entry from Angelina reveals:

> I notice that my partner was pay more atetion to the book about fish. I asked what she like about it and she said that she liked it because she was still interested in fish and she was going to make a play or some thing like that. I was glad that she was pay atetion beause I get mad when they don't pay atention.

This entry also illustrates how Angelina was beginning to make connections between students paying attention and the content of books being read. Choulaphone wrote about how she and the two younger students with whom she was working figured out words:

PHOTO 9    *Older students reflect after buddy reading.*

> The thing I learn from buddy reading that I knew that Mano and
> Mel remeber the words and when they go back to the words then I
> point to the old one and then they say it and they kept on doing
> that and when they come to a word they don't know then they ask
> me and I say alittle bit of the word and they just say it and just keep
> on reading.

Some students have expressed impatience with the emerging reading strategies of their buddy. In the case of Paul, he did not yet
understand the important role that re-reading favorite books can
play in the development of emerging readers, and shared his frustration at hearing the same story each week:

> Buddy reading was boring today because my buddy keeps reading
> the same book. He brings *Yuck Soup* [Cowley 1987g] every week.

Students may comment on changes, as María did when reflecting on
her buddy, Enrique. She wrote her reflections in Spanish:

> Yo haora me sentí muy bien porque hay algunos dias que Enrique
> no ponia atencíon y haora puso mucha atencíon al libro que yo
> escoge tambien a los que el escogio y tuvimos una largo discusíon
> cuando le leei mi libro. Hoy el estava prestando mucha atencion
> y cuando lo ivamos a empesar a leer le dije que si el queria leer o

yo y el me dijo "No se si pueda" pero yo le dije si puedes y empezo a leer aunque algunas palabras no las sabien muy bien pero al final la lleió perfecta mente.

(*Today I felt good because some days Enrique doesn't pay attention and today he paid a lot of attention to the book I chose as well as the books he chose and we had a long discussion when I read my book. Today he was paying a lot of attention and when I was going to start reading I asked him if he wanted to read or if he wanted me to read and he said, "I don't know if I can" but I said yes you can and he began to read although he didn't know some of the words very well but by the end he read it perfectly.*)

Some students may give a detailed commentary on their buddy's response to the books they read together, as Amphaivane did in the following entry:

My buddy always looked at the picture and when I ask her what she thought about the book she says something about the pictures. Like if I ask what she like about the book she says she likes the picture cause it looked real. When I read to her Cloudy and the chance of meatballs she said (after I was done reading) that the story is weird because food fell out of the sky. Then I asked her would she wished that it rained or snow food like in the Book and she said no cause the streets would be filled with food and it be dirty.

Sometimes, the entries describe discussions that followed a reading. Manuel often did this, and, in the following example, he wrote his entry in English, even though his native language is Spanish and he is still acquiring English:

What happen today in Buddy reading was Darron get a book the title was *In the Attic.* by: Hiawyn Oram Satoslti Kitamura [1984]. He like this book because when he go in the top of the roof there were I fManoly [a family] of mouse and when there were just the plants I aks hem If he will like to be in there By hi self and he say did you I tell hem yes he say me too. He say he would like to be in the story like the boy. Next book did I read was Each [Peach] Pear Plum by: Janet and Allan Ahlberg [1979]. I tink he like this book too because I aks hem what he would do If he found a Baby and he say he would tell his mom and picket up. He love when there were old [all] the people like in a party. he would like to do the same thing whit his famyly.

Gail encourages her students to write in whichever language they are most comfortable with. Some of the students who are most fluent in

Spanish elect to write in Spanish, as María did. Others, like Manuel, wrote in English. Manuel may have elected to write in English because most of his Spanish-speaking friends wrote in English; unlike him, however, they are most fluent in English.

When Kim Lon wrote her entry she focused on the very stimulating discussion she had engaged in:

> Buddy reading was very fun today. We also had alot of discussions.
> First we read *Lazy Mary* [Melser 1987]. Then I ask my buddy,
> "Do he every felt lazy?" First he said no then he said last night he
> couldn't go to sleep so he feel kind of lazy this morning. And I
> said, "What did your Mom or Dad did to you?" We had a very long
> discussions, but it would take me too long to write them down.

Sometimes the students' discussions range beyond simply reading a book and talking about it. On occasion, the books that are brought to the session spark a discussion before they are ever opened, as Tamara's comments illustrate:

> Today my buddy and I had a good time. Sangkhom read to me 1 of
> the books that he brought. And one of the books that I had also.
> But the book that I had was *The Living Ocean* [Cox 1989].
> Instead of him reading the book he told me what animals were.

Not all the children have a successful buddy reading experience and they share their frustrations and concerns in their logs. For example, Seng Orn began working with a new buddy and making the adjustment was not easy for her:

> Today I fell [felt] sad because my buddy she went to Laos and I
> have a new buddy and this buddy that I have today he does[n't]
> want me to read it him he said that he want to read by his seft
> [self] so I let him read by hiseft and was telling me about the book
> that he read by himseft. And he said that he very like this two
> book that I pick and write it down and draw it. And I have a little
> bit of problem because he don't even liste to me when I was read-
> ing to him.

Sometimes the older students are confronted by situations that they have no control over, such as when children come to buddy reading already in an upset state. This is always a difficult situation for any teacher to deal with, and the following entry from José Luis reflects how helpless he felt at not being able to help relieve Rhodora's unhappiness:

Mi libro favorito de hoy fue *The Birthday Cake* [Cowley 1987a], pero me fue mal proque Rhodora tenia sueno y se puso a llorar me senti triste no sabia que hacer porque ella no me queria decir lo que le pasaba y no me dijo se lo dijo la senorita. Ella se queria ir a casa.

(*Today my favorite book was* The Birthday Cake *[Cowley 1987a], but it [buddy reading] didn't go well because Rhodora was sleepy and she began to cry. I felt sad and didn't know what to do because she didn't want to tell me what was wrong or what the lady said to her. She wanted to go home.*)

Most students have difficulty from time to time getting the undivided attention of their younger buddies, and this concerns them, as the following entry from Esmeralda illustrates:

Today buddy reading went worser because my buddy was not paying attention and when I asked her something she would just say I don't know, I don't know, so I don't think that buddy reading went so well today because she also forgets to say some words that she allready knows just because she doesn't want to when I ask her to read some of the lines from the book that I read to her and I know that she can do better, but I guess that she doesn't feel like reading anymore and she's allways looking up the ceiling and all around the room.

Students will sometimes comment on how their own teaching strategies influence the attentiveness of their younger buddies. In the following entry, Magali recognizes how read-aloud strategies can influence the degree to which her buddy is engaged:

I liked my buddy reading because she lisends all the time. She makes a big discaushion when she wants to. When she lisens to the book is when I shang [change] my voises. And when I make it ixided [exciting] we Never have probems together.

Similarly, Lance recognizes that the positioning of a book and turn-taking can influence the success of a session:

Today I put the book right in the middle and he start read to me. We took turn reading too. Like he read one book I read one book.

The quiet time devoted to written reflection acts as a springboard for the oral debriefing session that follows (see Photo 10). These debriefing sessions are an invaluable way to recognize the older students' accomplishments, successes, concerns, and ideas. They are

PHOTO 10 *Debriefing session with older students.*

also occasions for the students to offer each other mutual support through talking about and exploring possible solutions to difficult situations. Usually the discussion begins with an exploration of successes and accomplishments. Class members then raise concerns and problems, which the class addresses as a group of interested colleagues. The written and oral debriefing sessions also underscore for the students the notion that the buddy reading program is a serious event in the school day, and that we take their comments and insights seriously.

In one debriefing session, María commented that her buddy, Enrique, didn't know if he could read, and she had told him "Yes, you can!" . . . and he then proceeded to read a whole book by himself. Gail asked the class to consider the strategies that María had used successfully with her buddy. Lance said, "She encouraged her buddy," to which Ana added, "She let him read and didn't read for him." Through this discussion, the class explored how important it is to encourage younger children to read, even though they may be hesitant. Later, in the debriefing session, Angelina commented that her buddy had paid attention, which had not happened often before. Gail asked her to think about reasons for such a change. After thinking for a few moments, Angelina said, "I think because it was a book about fish and she told me she liked fish." Once again, Gail asked the class to try to generalize from this experience: Why was this day's session so successful for Angelina? Vanessa offered, "She liked the book so she paid attention." Jesús suggested, "Find a book they're interested in. My buddy, Malcolm, likes snakes and when I read about them, he really listens good." In this way, the debriefing sessions move from identifying problems or new behaviors into the realm of making connections to teaching.

We have noticed that the content of log entries seems to change quite dramatically over the course of a year. At the beginning of the year, the first few entries are usually very positive and reflect a great deal of excitement. The following entry is what Barbara wrote after she first worked with her partner:

> Well Buddy Reading whent great. He could read very good and he really whanted to listen to the story he drawed very well and write good he wrote like this I LIK ET and I was really proud of him Well the book he mostly talked about more was the Three Billy Goats Gruff. He really likes book that has adventure and action he is great.

After a few weeks, though, the novelty seems to wear off, and entries are sometimes terse laments or complaints about the limitations of the younger buddies, as a later entry from Barbara illustrates:

> Well buddy reading whent a littel wild because my buddy was a littel wild. He didnt whant to read he just read one book and the rest of them he said they where all boring. I tried to tell him which book did he whant to read but he just kept on talking to Choulaphone and wouldn't let her read with her buddy we really didn't have a discussion going on at all well thats all.

We have noticed that students may begin to blame their younger buddies for whatever goes wrong. This seems to coincide with the pairs of children becoming more familiar with each other . . . but before the older students have learned a wide range of teaching strategies. After more time, the entries tend to move away from blame-placing to reflections on effective teaching strategies and students' accomplishments, as this third entry from Barbara, written later in the year, reveals:

> Well Buddy Reading today whent great he was really reading the book everey time I pointed to the think that it said in the book he will read it he felt very proud of himself and he wrote in his journal he wrote: I LK WN E WS OD TREE and I kept on encouragin him so he won't feel bad because he was kind of shy. Well my buddy payed attention 100%. he really was showing interest in the book. Me and my buddy din't have no problems at all.

In the beginning of the year, when suggested solutions are some-times thinly disguised threats, e.g., "Tell the teacher on them," "Tell 'em they 'sposed to LISTEN!" or "You can tell your buddy that if they don't pay attention, you're going to tell the teacher," Gail asks the class to consider how these suggestions will remedy the situation. That is, she encourages her students to think about underlying causes by asking questions such as, "Why do you think your buddy wasn't paying attention?" or "Is there anything you could do differently to keep your buddies interested?" This line of questioning seems to help the older children become more thoughtful, perceptive, and sensitive teachers. They become more aware of the impact of their role, and are less likely to immediately blame their buddies.

We have learned that problems presented and discussed at a debriefing session are often more complex than they initially appear. For example, at the beginning of the year, older students frequently comment on a lack of attentiveness on the part of the younger students. However, we also hear the first and second grad-ers commenting on how their fifth- and sixth-grade buddies some-times ignore them, or talk to their peers, or read in a monotonous voice, or pick books that are too long for a six-year-old. In our observations, we notice a very complex mix of factors influencing apparently inattentive behaviors. These conflicting insights lead us to make careful observations during buddy reading; they also influ-ence the focus of minilessons. For example, Gail has conducted minilessons that have been directed towards ways of capturing the younger children's interest (e.g., reading with expression, finding books that interest the buddies, engaging the younger children through discussion about the pictures, and giving encouragement). Problems are usually worked out quite well once students have been given opportunities to brainstorm possible causes as well as solu-tions. Providing the students with a forum for airing concerns as well as successes also validates their efforts as tutors.

We listen very carefully during these debriefing sessions as they provide us with invaluable information about the students' learning and development as teachers, the success of the program, and issues we need to follow up on in the future. The discussions and log entries frequently influence the content of future minilessons and issues that we focus on while observing. In this way, the debriefing sessions com-plement the observations that we make during buddy reading.

The debriefing sessions are stimulating sessions, filled with hon-esty, thoughtfulness, and information. However, we see ways in which this time to consciously reflect upon learning and teaching could be enhanced. For example, time constraints make it impossi-ble for us to address all the issues that students would like to discuss in the whole class debriefing sessions. Therefore, Gail is planning to set up weekly small group meetings in which students discuss their experiences and provide support to each other. In this way, we hope that all the students will have an opportunity to raise concerns or questions and receive feedback. One possibility is for students to meet in groups after they have written their reflections, but prior to the whole class sharing. Another option is to alternate whole class with small group debriefing sessions. Another change that Gail would like to implement is to read the students' logs on a more regular basis. Ideally, she would like to read every log each week, but suspects that she won't be able to handle this. Therefore, she plans on reading about six to eight logs each week, alternating the logs so that she reads each log more often. In this way, she hopes to be better in touch with the progress and needs of her students.

## ONGOING PREPARATION OF THE YOUNGER STUDENTS (THE TUTEES)

About a year ago, it dawned on us that the younger children did not seem to understand what their role was in buddy reading. This was true regardless of the developmental stage of the child. The first/second-grade class includes children who are very sophisticated, experienced readers and writers, and children who do not yet make extensive connections between oral and written language. Sammy is a good example of a child like this. He is lively and quick-witted and popular with the older children. His writing is limited to random letters and he reads from memory. Sung is very different. She is so quiet that Katharine and Gail aren't sure if they have ever heard her speak. She is a fluent reader and writes her own easily-decoded messages. Despite their differences, all the children needed to be better prepared for buddy reading. They are an integral part of the buddy pair and need to take responsibility for choosing books that they are able to read or are interested in hearing read to them. Similarly, they share responsibility for contributing to the book discussions. At first, Mary did very little in the way of preparing the younger children for buddy reading, but she has seen the benefits of using minilessons to provide focused teaching that is grounded in what she hears and sees during buddy reading. We also solicit student feedback on the program in debriefing sessions held at the end of each buddy reading session.

### Using Minilessons

The range of minilessons for the first and second graders tends to be narrower than for the older students, though similar themes are addressed throughout the year. Many issues are returned to more than once, but as the children become more skilled speakers, readers, and writers, the focus of these minilessons becomes more narrowly defined. Topics for minilessons in the first and second grade class are generated by what we observe during the buddy reading sessions and what we hear in the discussions held during the debriefing sessions. See Figure 10 for a list of minilessons taught last year. They have been organized into three categories:

1. *Procedural issues.* This involves choosing books and record keeping.
2. *Reading and writing strategies.* This includes bedtime reading strategies, and reading and writing skills and strategies.
3. *Social, interactional, and management issues.* This includes interactional and social skills.

---

**PROCEDURAL ISSUES:**
*RECORD KEEPING*
How to record the books you read
When to write and what to write
*CHOOSING BOOKS*
Where to find books
Choosing an appropriate book
**READING AND WRITING STRATEGIES:**
*BEDTIME READING STRATEGIES*
How to sit
How to hold a book
*SKILLS AND STRATEGIES*
Tracking when reading—when and how to track
Taking turns reading
Using pictures to help you read
*WRITING STRATEGIES*
Invented spelling—different ways to write
When to let your buddy help you write
The role of drawing in writing
**SOCIAL, INTERACTIONAL AND MANAGEMENT ISSUES:**
*INTERACTIONAL SKILLS*
Responding to buddy's questions
Sharing own responses to a book
Having a discussion after reading a book
*MANAGEMENT*
Sharing your buddy—creating a threesome when tutors are absent
Where to sit in the classroom
How to handle inattentiveness on the part of your buddy
*SOCIAL SKILLS*
Attentive listening
Showing respect for your buddy

---

Figure 10    *List of minilessons taught to first and second graders.*

In the following pages, we describe three minilessons that represent some of the more dominant issues that are addressed in this way. Although most of the minilessons are conducted with the whole class, Mary will occasionally meet with a small group (see Photo 11).

**Selecting books.** A recurring theme in minilessons is book selection, which Mary has found to be a critical element in a successful buddy reading session. Many of her students have not had much experience in carefully selecting books for reading aloud. On several occasions, we have noticed tensions developing between buddies when the younger students take books that do not really interest them or are too long. The older students would complain that the younger children were looking around the room, talking to other students and sometimes wandering around the room. If the tutor is a fluent reader and the story line is engaging, a new or longer text can lead to a very stimulating and engaging experience. However, tensions can develop when the text is too complex for an inexperienced older reader to read smoothly and with feeling. Similar tensions have arisen when younger students have selected books that did not interest them. One day we noticed how Oscar was stumbling a lot when reading to Waymond. It was clear that the reading experience was not very satisfying or successful for either of them. In the debriefing session, Waymond complained that buddy reading was boring because the book was too long. In the discussion that followed, we discovered that many students were simply selecting books

PHOTO 11   *Small group minilesson.*

randomly, without any regard for their interests or reading experience. Although some of the older, more experienced readers in the class already knew which features influenced their successful selection of books, Mary realized that she needed to deal with this issue in a minilesson. The next week the class discussed successful book selection strategies, which Mary listed on chart paper:

When selecting a book that *you* will read, choose a book that you:
- know well
- like
- can read

When choosing a book that you want *your buddy* to read to you, choose a book:
- that interests you *or*
- that you know and enjoy

Book selection is a topic that the class usually returns to on more than one occasion in the year.

When we noticed that the students seemed to be caught in a routine of selecting only one genre for buddy reading, storybooks, Mary used a minilesson to introduce the notion that poetry could be selected also. As part of the language arts program, the class is introduced to a new poem each week, which the children recite, chant, act out, and memorize. They also put together small tagboard puzzles, which are designed to help them learn the poem. These poem puzzles, which are stored in a large tub, are now a popular choice for buddy reading—the older students also enjoy them, seeming to appreciate revisiting familiar poems, many of which are old favorites.

**Participating in discussions.** Another topic that is usually returned to on more than one occasion is the importance of participating more during buddy reading book discussions. Many of the older children express frustration when the younger buddies do not respond to their questions, or mutter "I don't know," or simply shrug their shoulders. Successful buddy reading discussions depend upon both children contributing to the discussion, and this is a topic that the older students also explore throughout the year. However, it is a topic that needs considerable attention in the first-/second-grade classroom. In minilessons, Mary demonstrates different ways of responding to books. For example, one day she played the role of a younger buddy who was having a terse book discussion with her older buddy. In preparation for this minilesson, Mary had prompted one of the students, Mano, to ask her about her favorite character and what she liked about the book. Mano began by reading two pages from *The Little Red Hen* (Galdone 1973). Then she spoke to Mary:

MANO: Did you like the book?
MARY: [Nods her head]
MANO: What did you like about it?
MARY: [Shrugs her shoulders]
MANO: Who was your favorite character?
MARY: I dunno.

After this short, unsuccessful interaction, Mary asked the class, "What's the problem here?"

BILLY: You didn't talk.
MALCOLM: You need to answer the question.
MARY: How do you think Mano feels?
KHANH: Sad.
MARILYN: She feels bad because you won't talk about the book.
MARY: How did you feel, Mano?
MANO: Mad. And sad. You didn't say nothing.
MARY: That's right! After Mano read to me, I needed to talk to her about the book. I needed to tell her what I liked about the book, my favorite part or my favorite character, or point to the picture I liked best.

Mary then asked for a volunteer, one who could do a better job of discussing the book. Half a dozen children waved their hands in the air. Billy came to the front of the rug, where he joined Mano who read two more pages from *The Little Red Hen*. She then asked Billy what he liked about the book:

BILLY: I liked the part when the Little Red Hen ate the bread all by herself.
MANO: Why did you like that part?
BILLY: 'Cuz all the other animals had to watch her eat all the bread. They deserve it. They didn't help.
MANO: Who was your favorite character?
BILLY: I like the dog 'cuz he look funny sleeping. [He shows her the picture.]
MARY: Let's give Mano and Billy a big hand! They did a great job! How did you feel this time, Mano?
MANO: Good 'cuz Billy talk with me. He share his ideas about the book.

The children continued discussing what Billy had done to help keep the discussion going, which Mary recorded on chart paper in the form of guidance for the whole class:

- Tell what you like about the book
- Explain why you like the book
- Tell who your favorite character is

  - Explain why this is your favorite character
  - Show your favorite picture
  - Explain why it is your favorite picture


At the end of the minilesson, Mary reminded the children that they should remember what Billy had done so successfully and try out some of the strategies. Sometimes pairs of children practice these strategies with each other while reading familiar books together. This pairing frees Mary to sit with the few children who are still experiencing difficulties with book discussions. These children are usually beginning English speakers and Mary shows them how to use pointing and even a few words (e.g., "That's funny") to contribute to book discussions.

**Writing in logs.**   The children often need help when learning how to write responses to books in their literature logs. Many of them are beginning to crack the sound/symbol correspondence system of English writing, and after the first few buddy reading sessions, when the younger students have had practice in orally responding to books, Mary introduces them to written responses. A recent minilesson on the topic began this way:

MARY: Let's review the steps in buddy reading. What do we do first?

DARRON: Read to our buddy.

MARY: Then what?

KEOVONG: Our buddy read to us.

MANO: Then we talk about favorite book.

MARY: Good! You remembered all the steps! Today we're going to learn a new step. Here's a special notebook that you're going to use to write about your favorite books.

KARL: What if we can't write it? What do we do?

MARY: OK. Let's pretend I want to write about my favorite book, *The Gingerbread Boy* [Galdone 1975], but I don't think I can write. I want to write, "I liked the Gingerbread Boy because he ran away from lots of animals." [She picks up a piece of chalk and begins to write on the chalkboard] I know how to spell *I*. [She writes *I*] Like. Luh, luh, like [She stresses the first sound]. What sounds do you hear?

YIEN FOU:   El. [Mary writes *l*]

MARY: Like [This time she stresses the *k*]. What other sounds do you hear?

RHODORA: K. [Mary writes a *k*]

MARY: OK. We wrote *I like*. [She points to the words as she reads them aloud] The next word I want to write is *the*. Who's a *the* expert?

MALCOLM: T-H-E [Mary writes *the*]

MARY: "Gingerbread." That's a hard one for me. [She stresses the first sound in the word and writes *g*, followed by a dash] *Boy*. [She stresses the *b*]

MEL: I know. B-O-Y.

Mary continued writing in this way, stressing beginning and ending sounds in each word and leaving blanks where the children knew there should be a letter or letters, but could not articulate which letters corresponded with a given sound. After a couple of minutes, the following message was written on the board: *I lk the g_____ boy bks he rn a_____ fm ls v a_____* (I liked the gingerbread boy because he ran away from lots of animals.). Once she finished writing, Mary asked the class, "What did I do that helped me write the words in my literature log?" and the children begin to share their observations:

DARRON: You sound 'em out and write the letter you hear.

JARVIS: You put a line for the hard ones.

MANO: If you a expert, you write the whole word.

After this brief discussion, Mary reminded the children that during buddy reading everyone should draw a picture about their book and write as best they can about their favorite book and added, "Remember what we learned today. Show your buddy what you learned today as you write in your log."

## Using Debriefing Sessions

At the beginning of the year, the first and second graders meet on the rug immediately after the class has reconvened after buddy reading (see Photo 12). At that time they debrief via a discussion. Usually, the children share what happened and what they liked about the time they spent with their buddy partners. In the following excerpt from the beginning of a debriefing session, the children are sharing their experiences, "popcorn style," a strategy that many teachers use to encourage student talk:

MARY: How was buddy reading today? Let's put our hands down and think about how things went. [The children are silent for about thirty seconds and then the discussion begins.]

DANIELLE: I like to read. It's fun. My buddy's good. She likes me.

SAMUEL: It's good 'cuz I draw a picture and my buddy say it good.

MONICA: I liked my buddy because she reads more longer. He does a lot of stories.

PHOTO 12   *Debriefing session with younger students.*

MANO: I like my buddy 'cuz she draw good.

SAMMY: I like buddy reading because I like to read to my buddy reading and my buddy read to me.

LANCE: I like buddy reading 'cuz I reading long and my buddy didn't help much. Just a little.

SUNG: I like buddy reading because my buddy read to me and I read to her.

MALCOLM: I read *Each Peach Pear Plum* together and I take turns with him. I read one part and he reads one part.

MARY: It sounds like a good system.

MALCOLM: Uh huh.

The children also raise problems they encountered. Sometimes these problems are raised spontaneously, as when Sounthavy said, "[It was] Boring 'cuz the story was too much long." At such times, Mary may make a note to address the issue later, but on this occasion, she asked Sounthavy how he could make sure that future sessions wouldn't be boring. He thought for a few seconds, and then said, "Pick a short one." Usually, Mary makes sure that the children have an opportunity to raise concerns as she is then able to more thoroughly assess the effectiveness of the program and offer support, if needed. This sharing of problems sometimes evolves after she has asked the class to think about any problems they encountered, as this excerpt illustrates:

MARY: Are there any problems with buddy reading?
SOUNTHAVY: When he pick a book too long I get tired.
KINGSTON: He won't let me pick the book that I want to read.

At times like this, the students are encouraged to explore the issues in greater depth, and suggest ways to resolve the problems. Sometimes the solutions reside in the younger children themselves (e.g., needing to more carefully select books). At other times, the solution seems to involve the older buddy. When this happens, we make a point of observing the buddy pairs that are involved the next week to determine exactly what is happening. We also discuss these issues in our lunchtime meetings so that we are all aware of potential problems and are able to help the two groups of students work through real or perceived conflicts.

For the most part, Mary has tended to limit the debriefing opportunities to the oral domain, but sometimes she also invites the children to reflect upon their experiences through drawing and writing. Christopher used fairly conventional spelling when he wrote about how his buddy helped him.

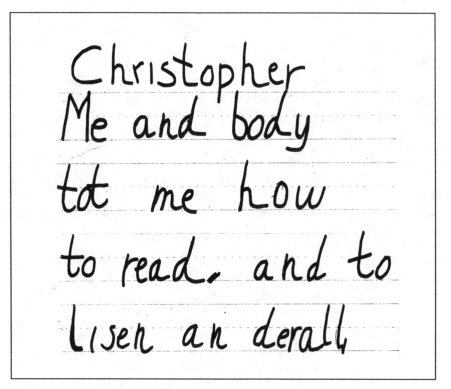

FIGURE 11    *Younger student's journal entry.*
Me and buddy taught me how to read. and to listen and draw.

When Kingston wrote a reflection to accompany his drawing, he used letters to represent distinct sounds:

ILKTUBYMYBTNYDFNFS.

(*I like to be with my buddy and we do fun things.*)

Sammy used randomly selected letters to accompany a drawing in which he and his buddy are holding pencils.

In the process of writing this book, Mary has had opportunities to reflect upon why she relies so heavily on oral reflection. The children are usually able to express themselves more fluently through the spoken word. However, time constraints inevitably limit the number of children who can make contributions in class discussions. This results in many children not having opportunities to share their thoughts and concerns with the rest of the class and Mary. This is where drawn and written reflections can be beneficial for both the students and the teacher. The children enjoy drawing and writing about their experiences, and through this domain Mary gains insights into her students' learning processes and experiences. It is not as if Mary thinks that these young children are incapable of writing or using drawings to think and reflect upon their experiences, as her class engages in journal writing and other forms of writing each day during writers' workshop. She sees how these experiences help the children make sense of their world on a daily basis. While revising this chapter, as we discussed these issues, it occurred to Mary that maybe she had been intimidated by the eloquence of the written reflections that the older students regularly wrote.

We are constantly scrutinizing all aspects of the buddy reading program, and we revise our expectations and classroom procedures accordingly. Mary plans on extending opportunities for her students to reflect upon their buddy reading experiences. In the coming months she will explore with them the most successful ways of using print to do this. Several options that she is considering include the following:

1. The children draw and write about their experiences after the oral debriefing.
2. The children draw and write about their experiences before the oral debriefing.
3. The children draw and write about their experiences before the oral debriefing and then share their insights in small groups only.
4. The children draw and write about their experiences before the oral debriefing and then share their insights in small groups and in a whole class oral debriefing.

## ROLE OF THE TEACHERS

This buddy reading program would probably have died an unremarkable death a long time ago if it weren't for the fact that Gail and Mary work together closely on other school-related projects and are equally interested in the buddy reading project. We believe that teachers must want to work together, and be equally enthusiastic about the project. Teamings should not be mandated by administrators because buddy reading takes a lot of commitment and cooperative work. Also, the two teachers should probably have a common vision and similar philosophy of teaching and learning. It seems to help if there is an already-established relationship involving respect for each other and willingness to resolve any conflicts that may arise. The teachers need to keep in close contact with each other, planning, sharing observations and insights, and discussing concerns. This collaboration can be mutually supportive for teachers. Teaching can be a very lonely occupation, even though we are surrounded by people every day. On buddy reading days, we look forward to getting together at lunch as soon as the students have left for the cafeteria. At this time, we discuss our observations over brownbag lunches —the notes we take are invaluable when we discuss what has occurred in the two rooms and plan minilessons for the following week. The importance of teacher reflection and how it guides us in our teaching will be explored more fully in Chapter Five.

We believe that teachers need to carefully observe buddy reading pairs and keep anecdotal records. After discussing Katharine's fieldnotes, Gail realized that she needed to take a more active role in preparing the children to teach, as it was clear that they needed help in supporting emergent readers and writers. Also, close observations alerted us to the fact that forty-five minute sessions were dragging on too long at the beginning of the year and children were losing their focus after about thirty minutes; we subsequently reduced the sessions to thirty minutes.

When the students are working in their pairs, Mary and Gail spend some of their time monitoring the two classes and making certain that the pairs are on task. This is especially true during the first ten minutes, as the children are settling into their places. Most pairs settle right in and are quickly engrossed in reading. Both teachers encourage the students to sit wherever they are comfortable. Some pairs prefer to lounge on the rug, using pillows to prop themselves up, while others always return to the same table week after week. Still others will occasionally take chairs outside when it is sunny. In the beginning of the year, both teachers are very attuned to whether the students are being attentive and showing respect for their buddies as they are very crucial behaviors for a successful program. The teachers move around the rooms, making notes when they observe interesting interactions and behaviors. They pay attention to the children's book choices, trying to figure out which books make particularly good choices. They also listen carefully to the content of the discussions. What is being discussed and how are the two children interacting? What are the dynamics? Are the pairs working? They also coach students on occasion, particularly when they notice an incident that seems ready to get out of hand.

The observational notes are very helpful in debriefing sessions because they provide authentic feedback to the children. We have found that it is much more effective to draw upon the exact words and actions of the students when making comments and giving feedback, instead of using general platitudes, e.g., "The class did really great today in buddy reading." For example, one day during a debriefing session, Gail referred to her notes and said she had been impressed with how Damlongsong had got his buddy interested in the book by asking him, "What do you think the book is going to be about?" The whole class, not just Damlongsong, listened very carefully to Gail as she said this; her comment led into a very interesting discussion about the effects of asking readers to predict before opening a book. When we use specific and detailed comments, the students are much more attentive. We think that this may be because they see that we are very interested in what they do, think, and say, which makes the feedback more meaningful and useful.

Since taking a more active observational role in the buddy reading sessions, we have discovered how important our role is in the successful implementation and maintenance of a buddy reading program. Gail and Mary once thought that a successful experience depended primarily on the students. They now see that what they do before, during, and after the weekly merging of the two classes also has a profound impact on what transpires. Careful observations lead to increased knowledge, which influences instructional decisions. And all of this influences how effectively the two groups of students work together in sharing and enjoying books.

## READING MATTER IN BOTH CLASSROOMS

We have discovered that both classrooms should have a fairly extensive collection of books and magazines oriented towards younger children. In this way, books are immediately available during buddy reading sessions. In addition, the children can prepare themselves for future sessions throughout the week. Although the upper-grade classroom did not originally have a wide selection of books appropriate for younger children, Gail has expanded it through a variety of means—e.g., borrowing from libraries, friends, and colleagues; raiding the school's book room; using book club bonus points; and bringing in her own books from home.

The children discovered the enlarged books, big books, as a buddy reading option on their own, and it has been a very successful addition to the program. About midway through last year, a few of the younger children began to select big books to bring with them to buddy reading. Pairs of children working in Gail's class would hurry across the patio outside and return with a large book. Their excitement infected other children who then followed suit. We have noticed that the less fluent older readers in Gail's class are most likely to choose these books. Other children never select them. Although the big books do not always have the richness of language and concepts that may be found in other picture books, their predictability and engaging storylines support less experienced readers. We have noticed that the size of the big books forces both children to hold the book and turn the page, a very physical way of keeping younger children focused. At the same time, the enlarged print enables both children to follow the text easily, something that does not always occur with texts that are longer, more dense, or have much smaller print.

We have also discovered how vital it is to have a variety of nonfiction books and magazines available. Mary has subscribed to *Ranger Rick, My Big Backyard,* and *Zoo Books* for many years and has an ample supply for the two classes. These magazines lend themselves to rich oral language experiences for both students. Both teachers have begun to extend their classroom libraries to include more nonfiction as so many of the children have expressed an interest in it. See the Appendix for a list of books that have worked well with our students. We have sorted the books according to the following categories: patterned language books (shorter and wordless texts), patterned language book series, books for more fluent readers, poems/rhymes/songs, and nonfiction books and magazines.

## ONE BUDDY READING PAIR AT WORK

On several occasions, Vanessa, a sixth grader, had mentioned in debriefing sessions that she had difficulties with her buddy, Danielle. One day she said, "My partner doesn't like to read and when I ask her what happened in this part she says, 'I don't know.' She's not paying attention." A stimulating class discussion followed as students offered Vanessa suggestions and tried to explain why a young child would express such disinterest. In response to a suggestion from one of her peers, Soheila, Vanessa said that they went to a quiet place, but still Danielle didn't pay attention. Tamara suggested that she take a new partner. After more discussion, Viliphone volunteered, "Maybe she has that disease that Yellow Bird has. A reading problem." This led to a discussion of dyslexia and a book that many of the children had read, *Yellow Bird and Me* (Hansen 1991), in which a main character has dyslexia and does not do well in school. Manuel suggested that the problem might be related to how the two children sat together, which led to a discussion of "bedtime reading" strategies and ways in which nonverbal behavior can influence the success of a buddy reading session. We talked about how a child's personal situation could influence his or her attitudes and behaviors. After Viliphone suggested to Vanessa that she get to know Danielle better, Vanessa volunteered, "I think she thinks I get frustrated at her." At this point in the discussion, we were able to begin to explore ways in which our behavior could influence the success of the buddy reading sessions.

In order to better understand Vanessa's dilemma and then help her, we decided to closely observe her working with Danielle for a couple of weeks. After a while, we realized that Vanessa's style of interaction could be influencing Danielle's behavior. For example, we noticed how Vanessa signalled disinterest in and irritation with Danielle through loud sighs, raising her eyes to the ceiling, tapping her finger on the table, correcting her errors when reading, and taking over Danielle's writing so that it would "look right." We also noticed that Danielle was not as difficult or disinterested in literacy as we had once assumed. One day, Vanessa began to tell Katharine about her personal problems. Danielle brought books over and started to read them, but Vanessa steadfastly ignored Danielle's attempts to gain her attention. She shrugged off the tugs at her sleeve as Danielle said, "Look, look what I've got here," completing the anecdote she was telling Katharine. Eventually Katharine gestured towards Danielle and Vanessa reluctantly returned her attention to her buddy. One book that the younger child read was a favorite, *Little Miss Muffett*, which she had partially memorized. Instead of reading "curds and whey," Danielle said, "curds and pie." "No," said Vanessa abruptly, "that's whey." Each time Danielle came to "whey" she would read "pie" and each time Vanessa would correct her in a voice that became increasingly more testy. As Danielle seemed to be getting discouraged, Katharine moved behind Vanessa and suggested in a whisper that she let Danielle read without interruption, that this story telling was a way for Danielle to learn how to read. Vanessa glanced up, grinned with a sheepish look on her face, said, "Okay," and listened to Danielle finish her rendition of the story without interruption, except to give encouragement with an occasional "Uh huh." When Danielle had closed the book, Vanessa said, "You really know this book, don't you!?" This was the first time that her tone had revealed appreciation for Danielle's efforts, and Danielle's smile seemed to reflect how even small amounts of praise can influence a person's willingness to take risks.

As we carefully observed Danielle and Vanessa working together, we realized that we were viewing a Danielle that we had not known before. We had all previously viewed her as a resistant learner and inexperienced reader. She had frustrated most adults who had worked with her. We wondered if we had been misreading Danielle, as Vanessa apparently had also. The picture we now saw was of a young child who was showing excitement toward reading. We immediately realized that we needed to address these issues with Vanessa and with the whole class, as we had noticed similarly unsupportive behaviors on the part of some of the other older children. In debriefing sessions we had also heard the younger children talk about buddy behaviors that they found unhelpful (e.g., their buddies talking with their peers). We wondered if the older students realized how their subtle actions and responses could have a negative impact on their buddies. We decided that it would be a good idea for Mary and Gail to model the contrast between unsupportive and supportive behavior in a role play.

In this role play, Gail played the part of the tutor and Mary took the part of the younger learner. Gail sat at the front of the room and Mary came skipping in excitedly, carrying a big book, *Just This Once* (Cowley 1987c).

MARY: Gail, Gail, I brought my favorite book.
GAIL: Great, Mary. Let's read it. Would you like to read it?
MARY: OK.

Mary started to read the book, "Mom, can the horse come on vacation with us . . .," but Gail quickly interrupted when she heard Mary read "horse" for "hippopotamus." "No, Mary," she chided, "it's not horse, it's hippopotamus." Mary continued reading, saying "hippopotamus" once, but returning to "horse" almost immediately. Gail corrected her several more times, each time with a distinct tone of impatience. She then bent her head down and to one side, peering at the front cover that was almost on Mary's knees, looking for the book's title and author. As Mary continued to read, Gail looked for a pencil, took out her journal and lifted the book up so that she could more clearly see the name of the author and title of the book. Mary continued reading, but her voice became less vibrant and clear. She was looking quite despondent when Gail said, "Wait! wait! wait! I have to write the title and author in my log." She interrupted Mary, took the book in her own hands and began to copy the book's title off the front cover. Mary lowered her head and shoulders, looking very crushed. When Gail had finished copying the title, she handed the book back to Mary and told her to continue reading. "No," said Mary, "I don't feel like it." Gail admonished her, "Come on, we're supposed to read. I want to hear you read." But Mary was adamant and said, "I don't feel like it anymore. I don't like this book."

At this point, Gail and Mary stopped the role play and opened it up for class discussion. "What's happening here?" asked Gail. The students pointed out how excited Mary was in the beginning and how she brought her favorite book; how Gail kept correcting her; how Gail was writing in her log when she should have been listening to Mary; and how Mary stopped wanting to read. They gave suggestions about how to improve the session, e.g., that Gail needed to listen while her partner was reading, should encourage her partner to hold the book with her, and shouldn't keep correcting her partner. Gail wrote these observations on the board and then she and Mary began another role play in which they demonstrated a more positive and successful interaction between two buddies. At the end of the role play, Gail summarized two important lessons she wanted the older buddies to pay attention to during buddy reading: to build on the younger student's enthusiasm, and to write in their logs at the appropriate time.

After the buddy reading session, when the two classrooms reverted back to their normal composition, Vanessa entered Gail's classroom with a broad smile on her face, the first time we had noticed such excitement after a buddy reading session. "Guess what! Danielle read seven books today!" she announced to Katharine. "Seven? What happened?" asked Katharine. Vanessa shrugged, but continued to smile infectiously. Katharine was moved by Vanessa's excitement as this was the first time that she had noticed her taking any pride in Danielle's accomplishments. In the debriefing session, Vanessa proudly shared her success with Danielle. "Danielle does like to read. She read seven books today." Gail asked her if she knew why there had been such a change in Danielle and Vanessa paused before saying, "I think it's 'cuz I was paying more attention. I let her read and gave her appreciations." "Um," said Gail, "What did you say?" "I didn't correct her when she said the wrong word and at the end I told her she was a good reader," she responded. Vanessa was noticeably more patient and interested in what Danielle was doing for the rest of the year, and they had a very successful relationship. Danielle began to take more risks as a reader and a writer. She attempted to write beginning sounds of certain words and began to self-correct when reading.

# 4

## "If It Weren't for Buddy Reading I'd Still Be Reading Bad."

## The Influence of Buddy Reading on the Students

Both the older and younger students have benefited enormously from buddy reading. Students tell us how the weekly experience has changed their reading and writing habits and processes. They comment on the new or increased pride they feel in themselves during buddy reading. We notice both subtle and dramatic changes in their behaviors—how formerly reticent children become more outgoing, how the more cautious are greater risk-takers, how perennial bullies reveal a nurturing side. We realize that a combination of many factors merge to influence such changes, some from within the school experience and some from without. Nevertheless, there is evidence to persuade us that the buddy reading program has had a significant and positive influence on the children. We will begin with how the buddy reading program has influenced the older children; we will then discuss the younger children.

### INFLUENCES ON THE OLDER STUDENTS

We have seen how buddy reading has led to some quite profound changes in the older students. Several of them have become more skilled and versatile readers. Many of their interpersonal skills have been enhanced. They all comment on how proud they are of their accomplishments with their buddies. Many of them reflect on what it means to be a teacher—they say that they have gained a new appreciation for the role of a teacher and relate these skills to their future lives as parents.

## Becoming More Skilled and Versatile Readers and Writers

A great deal of learning occurs when students assume the role of teacher, and the buddy reading program has provided the older students with an authentic situation in which to learn and practice skills and strategies that often make their own literacy experiences more successful. Because of the needs of the younger students, many of the weekly minilessons focus on beginning reading and writing strategies, e.g., using illustrations for clues to an unfamiliar word, using illustrations to predict what will happen next, or listening to the sounds in a word when trying to figure out how to spell it. Most of the students are very focused during the minilessons and we have seen how they immediately try to apply what they have learned to the buddy reading sessions that follow the minilessons. Every week the students also have the opportunity to read orally to their younger buddies. This oral reading practice helps improve the older students' fluency and understanding.

When reflecting in writing on how buddy reading has influenced them, several of the older students have commented on how it has helped them as readers. For example, Emery mentions how the practice of reading expressively to a younger buddy has helped him enjoy and better understand the books he reads:

> The way buddy reading has helped me in my reading is that if I read with more exitment and its funner to read and I start to enjoy the book and if I come to a word I can't read I just sound it out like I teach my buddy.

Norm comments on the helpfulness of a re-reading strategy that he learned about in a minilesson:

> Sometimes I don't understand a page in my littiture (literature) study book I jost keep on reading and when we have to go to a meeting we won't have anything to say. Then Ms. Whang told us that if your buddy doesn't understand a page read the page again. So I tryed that with my buddy and she started to tell me to read it again. I kind of frustrated but I didn't show it. Later when I was reading my book, I didn't understand a page so I tryed to read it again and it worked.

The buddy reading experience has provided a multitude of reading experiences that have led to improved reading fluency for many of the older students, as Angelina so succinctly captures in her comment, "I think it has helped me read faster because it is like practice for me and my buddy." Seng Orn writes about how, through buddy reading, she is learning beginning reading strategies over again, which contributes to her greater success and enjoyment as a reader:

> It help me because it look like I'm going back 1 grade and learn
> my ABC over and becasue reading is one thing that I like. And
> it help me more than I use to read from last year becasue I don't
> even no how to read that good like this year. So I say that this year
> help me more than last year.

Tamara, a fairly successful reader, believes that the buddy reading program has helped her to become a more patient, invested, and resourceful reader:

> Buddy reading has helped me to take the time when I read my own
> books. So like when I come across a word I don't look at the pic-
> tures because there isn't any. But sometimes I skip that word
> and read on or come back to it. At first I look at the book cover
> and think about what might is going to happen. And then I
> also read the back to also see what's going to happened. And then
> we also write just like them. We also write about the book. It has
> also helped me to not just look at a book and dosen't want to read
> it. And the Minnie Lessons has helped me to point and to follow
> along, so I would not get lost.

In the following entry, Barbara comments on having learned a lot of reading and writing strategies. Although she is not specific about all the strategies she has learned during buddy reading, she says that she has used many of them in her own reading. One strategy that she refers to explicitly is the importance of being persistent as a reader. In this entry, she also reflects on the importance of writing about things with which one is familiar:

> Well now that I teach I really learned alot of strategies. And when I
> am reading my own book I remember them and do what I
> remember. One time I was reading and I remember a strategie to
> stay put with the book to don't give up, to really understand and
> write my favorite stuff, put them in my literture booklet and write
> about it. And thats one of the things I teach in buddy reading. And
> I even do it in my own reading. I also learn and has helped me to
> when I don't understand a word to tell the teacher to give me what
> it meens or just find out by myself.

As the students reflect upon strategies that they use in their reading and writing, they are deepening their understanding of the strategies.

One of Gail's guiding principles as a teacher is that the highest form of learning is teaching. The buddy reading experience allows the older students to serve as teachers. As Derek says in a written reflection, "I think that doing this is really fun for me and the kids becasue I can pratice on my reading and learn how to be a teacher." Teaching a concept requires a deep understanding and the ability to break a concept down into parts. The older students put this maxim into practice when, as part of a study of Native Americans, they wrote concept books for their younger buddies about a self-selected Native American tribe. This writing experience obliged the students to synthesize ideas they had heard and read about, and write about them at a level a first grader could understand. Instead of copying from a book, they had to consider main points they wished to share, summarize the information and, on occasion, simplify the language so that it would be comprehensible to the younger students. On another occasion, the older students wrote picture books and big books for their buddies. In preparation for this writing, the students had to identify elements present in many of the picture books that their partners enjoyed and found success with. The fifth/sixth grade class generated a list of these elements, e.g., simple patterns, repetitive language, predictability, and manipulatives such as one finds in pop-up, slide and flip books. They also learned how easily and how simply they could present information about an insect or an animal using these formats. They learned that books do not have to begin with "Once upon a time. . . ." Candy, one of the least successful sixth grade readers, is an example of a student who became an enthusiastic reader and writer after making a book for her buddy. Although Candy is a struggling reader, the buddy reading program built on her strength as a caring and generous person. The wish to write a book for her buddy provided her with the motivation to go beyond her hesitancy as a reader and writer. She spent hours researching her topic, tracking down bookmaking resources, and writing. This noticeable change in Candy seemed to be connected to the authenticity of the writing task—she was writing for a clearly defined and familiar audience, which seemed to make the event relevant and engaging.

## Developing Social and Interpersonal Skills

Buddy reading offered the students opportunities to use and improve upon their ability to share, successfully interact, and work cooperatively with each other. These interpersonal skills include both verbal and more affective dimensions, such as having opportunities to nurture others. These were not outcomes that we had planned for, but were some of the most startling and revealing consequences. As Viliphone so poetically expresses in one of her reflections, "I think that the thing that I like best about the buddy reading program is that we get to open up each child when we talk about the book each week.'' Choulaphone reflects on the reaction of her buddy one day when she was late for buddy reading: "When I went to Ms. Pippitt class I saw her [Mano] all lonly and when I went in she was so happy that she saw me." Roberto comments on the relationship he established with his buddy: "Karl my buddy is reading good. I treet him like if he was my son and [he] treets me like a dad." Each of these students had clearly had an experience that fostered their nurturing skills.

Buddy reading offered the older students a rare opportunity to nurture younger children within the school day (see Photo 13). In most schools, the day and grade levels are so compartmentalized that students have few opportunities to develop these human qualities and skills. The program has given the younger children a much needed non-adult role model, someone in the same school whom they can look up to. At the same time, the older students have been encouraged to become nurturing and caring people, a role they don't often get to play in school and one that is often ridiculed by their peers. The weekly predictable encounter with younger children seemed to say to the older students that it is okay to look out for someone else and help out. Buddy reading was a relaxed, safe place for both students to share their feelings. One lesson that Amphaivane learned was "... you don't have to be shy of telling your feelings about the book to little kids. I've even learn that little kid's have

PHOTO 13    *Older buddy nurturing younger buddy.*

feelings of the book too." Some of the older students were convinced that the younger children shared their opinions more freely
with them (than with teachers) because they were closer in age.
Ronald comments about this in one of his written reflections:

> I think that the buddy reading program should continue because
> the 2 grader feel more comfortable working with us than the
> teacher becasue it make them feel better that they are reading with
> someone near the same age. They even talk more when they are
> meeting with us. They even understand more about the book that
> they are reading. Like I said, they feel more comfortable reading
> with kids near their age. When they read with grown up they don't
> feel so comfortable.

Although we were aware of how kind and skillful some of the students already were with younger relatives and neighbors, there were
several older students who had previously displayed only a tough
exterior. Some of the sixth-grade boys, in particular, surprised us by
the revelation over time of a new aspect to their characters. Whereas,
in the past, we had only seen the toughness in students like Jesús
and Juan (who sauntered around the school with a cocky and dispas-
sionate air, well aware of their power and mystique on the playground), in buddy reading we routinely saw a different, more com-
passionate and caring side to them. Walking around the classroom,
we would see Jesús with his arm affectionately wrapped around Malcolm, his first-grade buddy. We would glance around and see Juan
sitting close to his buddy, Keovong, listening carefully to and encouraging him as he read, totally oblivious to what was happening
around them. On other days, as we walked across the playground
over to the main building, we would sometimes notice how buddy
pairs were seeking out each other, just to check in and say hello.
Sometimes we saw how the older buddies would leave their own
games to play with the younger students or simply hang out together
until the end of the lunch period. One day Mano ran up to Mary
and proudly announced, "Look, my buddy let me wear her jacket. I
can wear it 'til recess is over!" These were new behaviors, the likes
of which we had rarely seen before.

Some of the students were already very skilled in their interactions
with younger children. Still, the buddy reading experience allowed
them to develop new skills and fine-tune their talents. One such
student was Angelina, who had immediately impressed us with the
degree of maturity and compassion she brought to her teaching. She
had a knack for being both firm and nurturing with the younger
children, particularly with some who routinely stretched us, children
like Khouanchith, whose reputation for unruly behavior had pre-
ceded him into first grade. At the beginning of the year, Khouanchith

seemed unable to focus on a task for very long, and Angelina talked about having a difficult time with him. She wrote about this in her log on more than one occasion:

> I[t] went okay, but I think he was shy being around a girl.
> (Nov. 30)

> My buddy talk alot, but he cainde [kind of] doesn't want to talk to me because I am a girl. So I tryed to make the best of it. I asked my buddy, "what do you think it is about" and he would say "I don't know" Well why don't you know? and then he would answer me.
> (Dec. 7)

Several weeks later, however, we noticed how relaxed and engaged Khouanchith had become during buddy reading. He and Angelina seemed to have established a successful partnership. We attributed this to Angelina's dedication to being an effective teacher—she would routinely try out new strategies discussed in minilessons or debriefing sessions. One day, Gail observed her using a discussion strategy, using funny questions, that she had learned from Damlong-song, one of her classmates. Angelina and Khouanchith had been reading *The Three Billy Goats Gruff* (Galdone 1981), and towards the beginning of the discussion, Angelina asked him, "Would you like to eat grass?" He shook his head, to which she replied, "Would you eat grass with catsup!?" Khouanchith laughed and the conversation took off. Angelina seemed able to get Khouanchith to do things we had rarely seen him do before. For example, one day they had been reading *Chicka Chicka Boom Boom* (Martin 1989), an ABC book, and Gail overheard Angelina coaxing Khouanchith into singing the alphabet song. Although Khouanchith refused to sing when with his peers or Mary, he eventually sang with Angelina. The one-on-one format of buddy reading and Angelina's widely-respected interpersonal skills apparently provided Khouanchith with a successful, nurturing experience, which benefited him. Thanks to Angelina's considerable interactional and teaching skills, Mary realized that Khouanchith's problems were not as serious as she had originally thought. She began to make sure that she made a personal connection with him at least once a day.

Buddy reading has also provided students with opportunities to engage in activities that encourage them to share and work cooperatively. For example, when the two classes made gingerbread houses, the pairs of students had to work together. While one buddy was holding the walls upright, the other applied icing glue. When the two did not work cooperatively, the houses collapsed. This activity also provided opportunities for the children to share. Many of the students brought in bags of candy, which they shared freely with each other. During the construction of the houses, we heard them making requests and suggestions, and offering candy: "Can I have a gummy bear?" "Use one of my candy canes for your fence around your house," and "Who has more M&M's that I can use for decorating my roof?" Children moved from one classroom to the other looking for the perfect candy to decorate their houses. We were impressed with the students' ability to share so freely.

The fifth and sixth graders have seen how the social skills of tutors can affect their buddies' learning. When another teacher asked the older students to give her own students advice on starting a buddy reading program, Vanessa wrote, "Try to get to know your buddy. Listen to there problems at home. Let them no that you want to be there friend." Jesús offered this advice, "Become friendship with buddy's maybe that will help." Through their responses, the students showed that they realized that good interpersonal skills are important for a successful buddy reading relationship.

A successful buddy reading experience depends to a great extent on the older students choosing books that the younger children enjoy, as Lance noted when he wrote, "Try to find out what kind of books do the buddys like." Barbara commented, "Pues que tenga libros de la perferiencis do los nino" (*Get books that the children like*). That is, in order to work successfully with the younger children, fifth and sixth graders need to get to know their younger buddies, and this requires fairly sophisticated listening and interactional skills. These are life-long skills that can be used both inside and outside the classroom.

## Improving Discussion Skills

Many of the minilessons throughout the year focus on strategies for encouraging discussions, as the older students often complain that their buddies won't talk about the books they read. The first and second graders will often shrug their shoulders and say, "I don't know," when asked what they think of a book. This is very frustrating for the older students, and it is a frustration that we can empathize with as we know first-hand how difficult it can be when students are unresponsive, e.g. during literature study circle discussions. Ronald commented on how difficult it can be when leading a discussion in the following excerpt from his log:

> It is really tough when you are trying to think of a question. There is a lot of question, but you can't think of just one. I wonder why it is hard to think of a question when there are hundreds of question. It is pretty hard being a teacher though.

We have explored many strategies for encouraging discussions, such as using open-ended questions, sharing one's own opinion about the book, and discussing the pictures while reading a book. We also focus on procedural issues, such as holding the book so both children can see it and taking turns reading, as these can influence the success of a discussion. These suggestions usually go a long way towards improving the quality of the buddy reading interactions. Through the weekly practice of being responsible for initiating and maintaining discussions, the older students get constant reinforcement in a skill which they then begin to incorporate into their discussions about books with their peers and teachers. We have noticed more and more participation in book discussions during the fifth- and sixth-grade language arts block, and several students have drawn on their teaching experiences to enhance their peer discussions. Barbara has learned that talking about how books affect her and responding to books through drawing are successful discussion strategies that she uses outside of buddy reading:

> Onother strategie that has helped me from buddy reading is to always put my own feelings about the book tell what made you mad. And also sometimes I do pictures of the think that was really sad for me or grosse.

Kim Lon wrote about how she has learned to prepare herself for book discussions by asking herself questions:

> What really helped me in my own reading from buddy reading is when I reminds my self about which more question that I have to ask myself like I was asking my buddy and start a conversation. So then I will start my own conversation myself and ask my self. That's how buddy reading helps me and I like that.

This year, Kim Lon has read many more books than she did in the past and, although she has some trouble with comprehension, she is an enthusiastic reader. She now actively participates in literature study group discussions and asks questions when she doesn't understand, something that she never did before. In a recent discussion of *Tuck Everlasting* (Babbitt 1987), Kim Lon disagreed with Angelina about an important event in the book. Suddenly, Kim Lon realized that she had misunderstood and asked Angelina to clarify for her. Once a very reticent member of group discussions, Kim Lon seems to have been helped by her buddy reading experiences to become a more confident member of discussions.

Through the buddy reading sessions, the students learn that listening carefully and attentively is a first step in starting a discussion. Denise commented on the importance of listening to her buddy:

> What I learned by working with the kids in buddy reading is that little kids have alot of opinions and sometimes they don't get to

talk about them. I learned how to be patient with kids and listen to
them When you pay attention to the kids they express more of
their ideas and I like to here their ideas aobut different books. My
favorite part was being a teacher bcasue I got to ask kids questions and observe that they were like and how talkative they were.

The students also learn about the most appropriate times to speak,
when to listen, and how to draw out responses from others. Magali
illustrated her ability to use this knowledge when talking about *Owl
At Home* (Lobel 1987) with her partner Khanh:

MAGALI: Have you ever seen snow?
KHANH: Yeah. [excitedly]
MAGALI: Is it cold?
KHANH: Yeah. Really cold.
MAGALI: I've never see snow before. I never touched snow before.

A stimulating discussion ensued as Khanh immediately became an
expert on snow and clearly took great pride and pleasure in sharing
her experiences with snow, which she had seen when visiting Reno,
Nevada, with her family. Gail has noticed that many of the older students are reluctant to say "I don't know" when they are with their
peers. However, we have noticed that in the buddy reading sessions, many of them are much more willing to admit that they don't
know, as the previous excerpt from Magali's conversation with
Khanh illustrates.

Another very important aspect to facilitating a discussion is providing enough wait time. Children, like adults, need time to think
and process a thought or question. Studies have shown that teachers
often do not provide enough time for children to think before
speaking. In the following log entry, Seng emphasized in a very profound way how important it is to give children time to respond:

I learn that you got to give them time to talk. They don't have to
just come right out and say it. You got to encourage them to
talk and say what they thought about it. I learn alot from this program. I learned that working with little kids are hard because
they don't have literature discussion in their classrooms. And I also
learned that they have a hard time talking sometimes because
their shy or maybe they didn't learned that theres no right
or wrong answeres in literature discussions so their afraid that they
might say the wrong thing. I also learned that if you want them to
talk you have to encourage them. You just can't expect to much
from them and you cant' expect them to just start talking when
they get to the table or rug.

The students recognize how important good discussions are for a successful buddy reading experience. In many cases, they incorporate strategies they hear about in minilessons into their conversations. In other cases, they come up with their own strategies for facilitating discussions. It is through their experiences that these strategies evolve and are fine-tuned.

### Becoming More Skilled at Making Book Selections

When the year begins, Gail asks her students to read fifty children's books in preparation for buddy reading. She asks the students to choose books that interest them and then evaluate them. Through this process, the fifth and sixth graders become aware of favorite authors, genres, and topics that interest them. Kim Lon chose *Chicken Soup With Rice* (Sendak 1986) to read with her buddy and wrote the following evaluation of the book.

> I choose *Chicken Soup With Rice* [Sendak 1986] because it's my favorite book and it ryhmes alot. And in every pages its short and ryhmes. I think my buddy Dereks would like ryhme book. I also chose *In The Dark, Dark Room* [Schwartz 1984] because I think that my buddy would like it becasue he always asked me for a scary story. I think for myself is not scary, but the my buddy I knew it is scary. And he would love to read along with me becasue he sort of know the book already.

When Emery evaluated his selection, he reflected on how books can stimulate thinking about one's own life:

> I choose *Alexander and the Terrible, Horrible, No Good, Very Bad Day* [Viorst 1976]. Its a funny book too. He mite like it because maybe he had a bad day just like the boy in the book and if he did he mite pay more atenntion to the book. He mite listen and find out what the boy did to feel better and he mite try what the boy did to fell better when he was having a bad day."

Later in the year, Soheila revealed knowledge about her buddy's book preferences when she selected a book with a happy ending: "I think my buddy will like this book because it has a happy ending and she likes 'happy' stories." Aromrack chose a book that teaches a lesson she felt was important for younger children to learn: "I chose *Jump In Now!* because it's gonna teach little kids not to go in water without an adult." María has learned that Enrique likes animal books and books that have happy endings:

Yo use este libro proque a Enrique le gustan mucho los libros de animales y que no sean muy largos, ni muy cortos y este libro es de unos puerquitos y no esta muy largo. Y tambien a Enrique le gusta que empiese triste y que se acave feliz.

(*I used this book because Enrique likes books about animals, and books that aren't too short or too long, and this book is about little pigs and it's not very long. And Enrique also likes them to begin sad and end happy.*)

Possibly as a consequence of these opportunities to select and then evaluate books, the older students begin to apply what may be new information and strategies to their own reading. They become more conscious about genres they like and dislike, and during their literature study discussion groups, now exclaim that they want to read a humorous book, an adventure story, or a mystery. They are also now more likely to talk about favorite authors of books for young adults, the most popular of which are Roald Dahl, Judy Blume, Walter Dean Myers, Candy Dawson Boyd, Gary Soto, and Yoshiko Uchida. Through the active process of carefully selecting books each week for buddy reading and being able to talk about influences on those selections, the older students are becoming more aware of their literary likes and dislikes.

## Becoming Knowledgeable About Picture Books

Many picture books are written so well that they appeal to and/or challenge older readers. Unfortunately, though, there is a prevailing belief in many schools and among many upper-grade teachers and students that picture books are inappropriate reading matter for older students. Consequently, it is not uncommon to find that older children are self-conscious about reading picture books and are afraid that they will be teased or ridiculed if they do so. As a result, they are, in effect, denied access to some fine stories, fascinating themes, and spectacular illustrations. Many picture books can provide a very successful reading experience for students, particularly the less experienced readers and those who are acquiring English as a nonnative language, because they are shorter and have pictures which aid in understanding. Damlongsong expressed this sentiment in the following end-of-year reflection:

Buddy reading help me read better because I get pratis with him and I get to read pitcre [picture] book because in the class I read chapter book with no pitcre and some of the book get boring because I don't see no pictur.

We have found that the older students get a great deal from the picture books that they read for buddy reading (see Photo 14). Animated discussions have followed the reading of books such as *The Tiny Seed* (Carle 1987), *Bringing the Rain to Kapiti Plain* (Aardema 1981), and *Follow the Drinking Gourd* (Winter 1988).

## Learning Read-aloud Strategies

In the buddy reading program, the older students learn many strategies for successfully sharing books with a younger child (see Photo 15). These basic strategies are critical to both buddies enjoying books together. We have seen how learning to read aloud effectively enhances the older students' understanding of the stories they read and the characters they encounter in both picture books and young adult novels. In minilessons, Gail emphasizes many read-aloud strategies, including the following: reading with expression, when to alter one's tone of voice, when to read dramatically, how to verbally and non-verbally convey a character in a book, and how to create the atmosphere suggested by a story. Through these lessons, the students build upon their understanding of a story. They are also learning how to captivate their audience. Viliphone, a fluent and avid reader, commented on how having practice in reading aloud had helped her read more fluently and with greater understanding:

PHOTO 14    *Older student engaged in an animated discussion about a picture book.*

PHOTO 15    *Learning through practice how to share a book.*

It helped my reading alot. It helped me to read more. I like it
'cause it helps me read out loud to people more. It helps me read
with more and more expression. If it were'nt for buddy reading, I
would still be reading bad. I think that it has helped improve my
reading skills. So I like it alot. Now I know more words and I
can read better and better.

As a class project one semester, students made puppets of characters from favorite books, which they used as props while telling their
stories to their buddies (see Photo 16). Later, some of the students
put on a puppet show for an excited audience made up of first, second, fifth and sixth graders. Curious George, the Little Red Hen,
Madeleine, a crocodile, Clifford, Goldilocks, the Big Billy Goat
Gruff, and the Troll all came to life. All the children chimed in,
"Not I," during *The Little Red Hen* (McQueen 1985). When the Troll
was butted off the bridge during the performance of *The Three Billy
Goats Gruff* (Galdone 1981), screams of glee could be heard throughout the room. Gail commented later that her students would never
have responded in such an uninhibited way in front of their peers.
Through this puppet show, the older students were provided with a
natural setting and appreciative audience with which to practice and
improve on their delivery of a story. In one debriefing session, Damlongsong pointed out that in order to keep a younger buddy interested, "You need to become the character in the book." We believe

Photo 16    *Using a puppet to tell a story.*

that if children have opportunities to read expressively and dramatically, comprehension will improve.

## Improving Self-esteem

Like other teachers who are concerned about the lowered self-esteem of students who are not very successful in school, we are aware of the impact that increased self-esteem in one area can have on students' performance in other areas. Over the years, we have seen how lack of experience or success with reading can have a paralyzing impact on the success of students in school. It can be difficult to find risk-free situations in which struggling older readers have successful reading experiences. Buddy reading can provide such a risk-free environment that a successful experience can almost be guaranteed for even the least experienced reader. We have seen dramatic changes in how some of these students feel towards reading as a consequence of the buddy reading experience. After a few months, students who used to read for only a few minutes at one sitting before getting distracted, now read independently for forty-five minutes. We have seen changes in how the students evaluate their own reading ability. In a reading survey done at the beginning of the year, Lance wrote the following, "I think I'm not a successful reader because sometimes I think its boring or I don't know a word or don't understan." At the end of the year, Lance, whose attitude towards reading changed dramatically, commented on how buddy reading had helped him: "I could get more practice on my reading on buddy reading. And now every Saturday my dad brins me to the library to read books or check out book." As Derek reflected back on his year in the buddy reading program, he succinctly commented, "It made me read like one to thirty books a year. So That's all I have to say. Thank you!!!" Antoine wrote, "It incurrage me start reading books by myself," and Amphaivane referred to how she has become a much more confident reader:

> Last year I hated reading but this year when I follow advice from other people I've become so proud of my self for reading and when I read I feel so happy!!

In the following comment, Vanessa talked about how she learned how to work with younger children and that she learned from her buddy as well. It is apparent that her self-esteem has been raised through her work as a buddy reading tutor:

> Because I think that little books help me to read the bigger books easier. And what I learned from buddy reading is how to work with kids. It kind of gave me time to get to know my buddy and to feel good about our selfs. I like what I learned from my buddy. I taught her somethings and she taught me somethings and if I were to be a teacher I would love to have my students teach me a few things to.

## Using English in Natural Settings

This year Gail has many students who are still in the process of acquiring English. Five of them speak very little English, and they read books in Spanish. Because there are no Spanish-speaking students in the first/second grade class, they must share books in English during buddy reading. It has turned out to be a very effective way for them to listen to and use English in a relatively stress-free context. Before each session, Paco, José Luis, Deborah, Mara and Alonzo choose the books that they want to read to their buddies. They have begun with simple predictable books and first practice with a peer tutor. After listening to these books being read to them, they then practice reading aloud to each other. On one other occasion during the week, they practice reading aloud with each other and with other, more fluent English-speaking peers. During the week they also take home tape recorders, picture books, and audio tapes of the story to practice listening and reading in English. Because they are rehearsing for a session which happens on a regular basis with another person, the students are very diligent about reading the books over and over again. We had noticed how José Luis was becoming more self-assured and analytical during the buddy reading meetings, and one day, he told Gail that the book that he was reading was too easy and that he wanted a more difficult book with more words. He wrote in a recent log entry:

> El dia de hoy me fue my bien con Buddy Reading proque yo estaba nervioso pero me gusto y ya no estoy nervioso. Me companera de Buddy Reading yo pienso que esta en el paso que sabe algunas palabras.
>
> (*Today Buddy Reading went well because I was nervous but I liked it and now I'm not nervous. I think that my buddy is in the stage of knowing some words.*)

The buddy reading experience offers students who are acquiring English an authentic opportunity to speak and write in English. During buddy reading, students focus on the content of the books rather than grammatical forms or vocabulary forms, as is still often the case in ESOL (English to Speakers of Other Languages) classes. This informal setting seems to free up the least fluent English speakers to process the language and use as much English as they are able at that time. The fact that the older students are also in an expert role during buddy reading (as opposed to the novice role they often occupy while they are learning English) seems to contribute to a greater level of comfort, confidence, and sense of accomplishment.

There are many ways in which the fifth and sixth grade students have been changed by their experience of working on a weekly basis with a younger learner. The words they use themselves when describing the impact of buddy reading on their development as readers, teachers, and social beings (such as those we have included in the preceding pages) provide quite compelling examples.

## INFLUENCES ON THE YOUNGER STUDENTS

The younger children have also benefited in many ways from buddy reading. In addition to learning about and having experiences with reading and writing, they have also learned about successful ways of interacting with others. The younger students have been particularly influenced by the buddy reading program in the following ways:

### Learning to Use a Range of Reading Strategies

The first graders especially are just beginning their journey into the world of reading, and they benefit from all the encouragement and reinforcement they can get. They learn to listen when hearing stories being read aloud to them. They get practice in responding to books. They learn to read to and with other people. During the buddy reading sessions, the younger children have a chance to practice intensively many of the reading skills and strategies that they have learned in class, for example, using their fingers to track a line of print from left to right. With the help of their buddies, they make predictions and test them as the story is read. They review their knowledge of letters and sounds as they begin to use word identification strategies. The buddy reading sessions help them to internalize beginning reading strategies.

Once the first and second graders get to know their older buddies and establish a working relationship, they are able to read and write in a fairly risk-free situation, which seems to encourage them to try a variety of strategies. Because the fifth- and sixth-grade students have received instruction on the same emerging reading and writing strategies in minilessons, they are able to guide and reinforce the efforts of their younger buddies. When Roberto reflected on the accomplishments of his younger buddy, Karl, he mentioned emerging reading strategies that both classes had explored: think about the word first (to see if you can gets its meaning from context) and then try sounding it out:

> He read good. He didnot make eny mistakes. He improve reading He read every time. (If) He did not now the word he wount tell me to tell him he will think and sound out the word.

Mary teaches her students to use pictures to help figure out what a book is about. In the case of students who are not yet making sound/symbol relationships, this is a particularly critical strategy to use as they become more experienced readers. Sixth grader Paul commented in his log on how San Ching used this reading strategy quite effectively: "Buddy reading was fun. My buddy is telling the story by looking at the pictures."

When older students are able to work with the same student for two years, they frequently notice how their buddy's range of reading strategies change, as the following log entry from Choulaphone illustrates: "When my buddy readed I was shocked because my buddy readed the whole book without my help. Last year I really had to help her alot." The older students often comment on the reading and writing strategies that their buddies use from week to week. George remarked upon how his buddy, Darron, was becoming a more fluent and motivated reader: "Today buddy reading went great. He was in a hurry to read. He reads faster. Everytime I go back he is more eager to read."

## Learning Book Handling Skills

Book handling skills are crucial for a successful and enjoyable shared reading experience. If even one participant cannot see the pictures in a book, there are likely to be problems. In buddy reading, the children have talked about and practiced how to share a book—where to place the book, who turns the page, who points to the words, who reads, and how to take turns reading. These seemingly small details become important to the success of a reading session and lead to a better understanding overall of sharing and turn-taking. We have noticed how the younger students become more aware of their older buddies' need to see the page when being read to—instead of holding the book so that only they can see the words and illustrations, they begin to offer a corner for the older buddy to hold or put the book between them. They also become more willing to turn the pages where appropriate. We have seen many first and second graders who are not yet independent readers quickly glance up from the page, as if waiting for a clue from their buddy that the time has arrived for them to turn the page.

## Becoming More Skilled at Book Selection

The younger children are now much more aware of the kinds of books they enjoy, particular authors they like, and the optimal length of book that they enjoy hearing. Mary has tried to store the books in her classroom in a way that will help the children locate their favorite books. She wants them to be able to independently select their books for buddy reading. Because thoughtful book selections are a critical element in a successful buddy reading partnership, Mary listens carefully to their conversations while they are choosing books. Are they being specific in their choices? Do they know which books they want to take? Do they know where to find their books? One day, when she overheard Janice ask, "Where's *Huggles' Breakfast?* (Cowley 1987b) It's not in the basket!" she knew that Janice was not selecting books randomly. The same was true when Eata came up to Mary carrying an empty brown basket with a worried look and said, "No books. No *Huggles.* No *Birthday Cake* (Cowley 1987a)." She was close to tears as she could not find the only two books she felt confident about reading on her own. Mary looked around the room and saw that Malcolm was holding three books, two of which were those that Eata had been searching for. Since Malcolm was able to read more complex texts than those in his arms, Mary explained Eata's situation to him, asked if he would be willing to give one of the books to Eata, and encouraged him to select a slightly harder book. Malcolm spent a few moments considering Mary's request and suggestion, offered a book to Eata (who was delighted), and raced back to the class library to find a replacement.

In order to further ensure that the students are thinking about what books they are choosing, either to read to their buddies or to have read aloud by their buddies, Mary asks the children to talk about their selections. One day, Jenny proudly showed her selections to Mary and said, "I have *The Birthday Cake* (Cowley 1987a) and *Yuck Soup* (Cowley 1987g). I can read them!" After congratulating Jenny on carefully selecting books that she could read on her own, Mary gently reminded her to also find a book for her buddy to read. Jenny returned to a book bin and after pulling out three more books, eventually decided on a Dr. Seuss book, her favorite author.

Most of the more fluent emerging readers in the class particularly enjoy reading the books in two series of books, the *I Can Read Books* and *The Beginner Books*, which are stored in their own bins in the library corner. As the children rush towards the library corner to make buddy reading selections, they often argue with each other over who can take the current favorites, which are likely to include *The Berenstain Bears and the Spooky Old Tree* (Berenstain and Berenstain 1978), *Bears in the Night* (Berenstain and Berenstain 1978), *Are You My Mother?* (Eastman 1960), *Go Dog Go* (Eastman 1961), and *One Fish Two Fish Red Fish Blue Fish* (Seuss 1960). These books are quite a bit longer than books in other series intended for beginning readers (e.g., *The Sunshine Books*), but they are still manageable for emerging readers who can handle a longer text. Other favorites are books that Mary has read to the children during the day and books from the theme box (books related to the unit that the class is working on). Recently, the children were all scrambling to get the Hansel and Gretel books which were in the box, as the class was engaged in a mini-unit on fairy tales.

At the beginning of the year, before the children have had much experience in or orientation to selecting books, they will frequently pick books that are either too long or do not capture their interest. As the year progresses, this continues to happen on occasion, and, during debriefing sessions, the children will express their frustrations. When Danny said one day, "(Buddy Reading was) boring 'cuz the story was too much long," Mary asked him what he could do differently next week to avoid the problem. He replied, "Pick a short one." In the debriefing sessions, and then in subsequent minilessons, the children raise concerns surrounding book selection and find solutions. Generally speaking, though, as the year progresses, we notice that the younger children make thoughtful book choices. They know the books that they can read and they know where to find them. They are also aware of the kinds of books they like and choose these genres when picking books for buddy reading.

## Getting Practice in Reading to Others

Research shows that the single most effective way to help children with their reading is to read with them every day (*Becoming a Nation of Readers* 1984; Chomsky 1972; Durkin 1966). We also think that it is important for students to have opportunities to read to others as often as possible. Although Mary reads aloud at least two times each day, she does so to the whole class. Buddy reading provides all the children with a weekly opportunity to read in a more intimate and individualized way. During their regular debriefing sessions, the younger children frequently comment on how much they enjoy reading to their buddies. Monica said one day, "It's fun to read with my buddy. She let me read. She help me spell by sounding the words out with me." On another day, Malcolm commented, "I read *Blue Sea* (Kalan 1979) together and I take turns with him. I read one part and he read one part. I like that we take turns (reading) 'cuz then we don't fuss." Although the children are usually not very experienced readers, they take pride in their accomplishments, as the following comment from Lance illustrates: "I like buddy reading because I read long and my buddy didn't help much. Just a little." This opportunity to read to another person is so important to the children that they will complain if they don't get a chance to read to their buddy, as Quan did when commenting, "My buddy don't let me read. I want to read too." Enthusiasm for reading and confidence in themselves as readers are two eventualities that we are very interested in fostering, and having opportunities to read to a buddy seems to reinforce them.

## Becoming More Confident Writers

The first and second graders in Mary's class write often and for many purposes. On most days they write in their journals or at a computer during writers' workshop. Their topics are self-selected and they keep a list of favorites in their writing folders. Each child in the class has a pen-pal in Carson City, Nevada and they exchange letters on a regular basis. The children's excitement about letter writing has prompted Mary to construct individual mailboxes for each class member.

Often, especially in the beginning of the year, children will express concern over their perceived inability to spell conventionally, and will refuse to write. Mary encourages them to draw pictures and write whatever they can. She models writing on a regular basis and uses minilessons to show them how young people of the same age write differently and young people's writing changes over time. Although many children jump into recording their thoughts on paper through pictures, letters, and other symbols, other children are not so confident. The one-on-one attention that the older students offer during buddy reading seems to help all the first and second graders as they make that leap into the world of writing (see Photo 17).

The older students have learned to help the younger children become more independent writers, and they regularly encourage their buddies to listen to the sounds they hear in a word. One day during journal writing time, Monica and Lakeisha, both first graders, were talking together. Monica, not a very experienced reader or writer, stood over Lakeisha with a huge smile and sparkling eyes and

PHOTO 17   *Helping a younger student become a more confident writer.*

offered the following advice to her friend: "Writing is real easy. You just listen to the sounds and say the word and write the letters you hear. Like 'water.'" Monica said *water* slowly, emphasizing the dominant sounds, and continued with her advice, "See, the 'w' and a 't' and a 'r.'" Monica spoke with authority and confidence and Lakeisha matter-of-factly wrote *wtr*. This is the kind of advice that Monica receives on a weekly basis from her buddy, Denise, as she is writing in her literature log about a book they have read together. At the beginning of the year, Monica was extremely hesitant about her writing. She didn't take risks. In fact, she didn't write anything. Each day during journal time Monica would complain, "I can't write! I don't know how!" and was quick to ask adults in the room to spell words for her. Through the support offered by her teacher, classmates and reading buddy, Monica moved from seeing herself as a non-writer to one able to offer advice.

A similar situation involved Manop, a very timid and anxious first grader who was easily reduced to tears at the slightest provocation. During writers' workshop, Mary often saw him crying silently while sitting at his table. He was afraid to make the slightest mistake and the most he wrote during a thirty-minute period was an "I," and this was with Mary's assistance. The guided writing sessions that they had together seemed to help him a little, and he began to write beginning sounds, as in "I l_____ h_____" (*I like horses*). Gail was aware of Mary's concern about Manop, and one day, after reading a journal entry written by Manop's buddy, Barbara, she crossed the patio with the log and said, "Mary, look at this! Is this the Manop you were worried about? Look what Barbara wrote in her journal." Barbara had written the following entry:

> Well Buddy Reading today whent great. He was really reading the book everey time I pointed to the thing that it said in the book he will read it. He felt very proud of himself and he wrote in his journal he wrote:
> I LK WN E WS OD TRee
> And I kept on encouragin him so he won't feel bad because he was kind of shy.

Although the effects of buddy reading cannot be clearly isolated from other influences on their development as readers and writers, the younger children are clearly writing much more under the guidance of the older students. Mary believes that the weekly one-on-one "guided writing" that the older students provide is making a difference for children like Manop.

## Becoming More Skilled Conversationalists

Many of the younger children are very quiet during class or small book discussions. At times, their quietness can be a challenge for their buddy reading partners. Through observing and participating in role plays, the younger children see how difficult it is if all participants in a book experience do not offer their opinions or reactions. Throughout the year, we coordinate minilessons so that both groups of students learn discussion strategies. As the students become more accustomed to talking about books, the discussions tend to become more satisfying. We asked the older students to evaluate the buddy reading program, and several commented on how their buddies had become more effective members of discussions. Denise commented on how familiarity with the buddy reading program probably influenced her buddy's progress:

> I think that this program has help by getting kids to like the books better and read more. It's helped kids that are quiet to speak up more. I really think thats helped because my buddie would only answer a question if I ask her and now she answer alot of people. Now that the kids understand how the buddy reading program their not scared to share their opinions with us.

Nam expressed his belief that the younger children were more willing to talk with their older buddies because they are all "kids":

The buddy reading group is important because the kid is depending on us to teach them how to read and write. And some of the childrens doesn't want to talk to the teacher because sometime they are afraid of the teacher. So that's why it's importent to have buddy reading next year because the kid would more likely talk to us kid then the teacher.

Seng remarked on how she believed that the buddy reading experience would help the younger children speak up more readily in their classroom discussions:

I think that the discussions we had with them really helped them in talking in the classroom more because if they were shy the discsusions help them alot becasue now they probable speak up more in class.

## Developing Interactional Skills

Reading for young people is often a social act, and buddy reading builds upon that reality by offering interactive experiences for the first and second graders in a context that they understand and where they have the focused attention of their buddies. The conversations that evolve are natural and grounded in shared experiences. They are also fairly predictable as buddy reading becomes a familiar routine. These elements are particularly important for children who are acquiring English as a nonnative language as they need a nonthreatening environment in which to use their new language.

At various times during the year, the buddy reading pairs collaborate on an activity in their work sessions. For example, the older students have helped the younger children make intricate haunted houses, delicate lacy snowflakes, and gingerbread houses. Building the gingerbread houses was both the culmination of a unit on fairy tales and a holiday project. When the younger students reflected on the experience, many of them commented on the collaborative nature of the activity, as the reflection written by Yien Fou (Figure 12) illustrates.

When Karl wrote about the experience, he commented on how much he had appreciated how his buddy had helped him: "My house/ I.like. the. wae. my.bady. heept. me. do. my. house. and. we. dote.candy."

When the two groups of students are working together in this way, they have a natural context in which to have a conversation. One day, when the students were making haunted houses with intricate cut-out windows, we walked around the rooms and heard how the experience was helping to support the language development and interactional skills of the children. We heard newcomers to English

The Gingerbread boy House

I Make my House and my buddy too.
My Buddy Help Me. And I Help My Buddy
My buddy is a Girl. And I Put 8
And I Put Foop Loop. And I put 4 m. And
I use the Ice Glue. And it was
lot of fun. With my Buddy.

FIGURE 12    *Younger student reflects on collaborating with older buddy.*

express opinions, make suggestions, and ask questions, as the following remarks illustrate: "Put spider in window," "How make ghost?" and "I want put two pumpkin on step." This is the kind of support that children need as they begin to interact with others using a newly acquired language.

Through the buddy reading encounters, the younger children learn how to talk with other people and how to successfully interact with older children. As the year progresses, many of the pairs are mutually supportive of each other, both in the classroom and on the schoolyard. By the end of the year, it is clear that a community of learners has been established, a community that benefits the learning of both the older and younger students.

# 5

## "I Had No Idea That Manop Could Read So Well Independently."

## The Influence of Buddy Reading on the Teachers

In educational circles, the focus of discussion is usually the students, as it should be. We have seen how a buddy reading program can have a profound impact on elementary students. However, we have also seen how the experience has had an equally profound impact on all three of us, as teachers and as learners. We have learned strategies for better assessing and addressing the academic and affective needs of students. We have learned more about ourselves as teachers (e.g., influences on our practice, concerns we have, and changes that we would like to make). The buddy reading program has made us more reflective teachers. It has also contributed to us feeling a greater enthusiasm for teaching as we now have a deeper understanding of children's learning processes and our role as teachers in enhancing their learning. This influence on us has been profound and far-reaching, and it is something that we would like to share with other teachers in a spirit of professional collegiality.

We would like to explore some of the ways we have been influenced through the buddy reading program. This is by no means a completed journey. We are continually learning and making changes in our teaching practices as we discuss and reflect together. In fact, the process of writing this book has helped us refine our theories of how children's language and literacy development evolve, and this, in turn, influences our practice. We would like to explore in greater detail some areas in which we have been most profoundly influenced by the buddy reading program.

## TEACHING READING STRATEGIES TO
## INEXPERIENCED OLDER READERS

About half of Gail's fifth- and sixth-grade students are struggling readers who have a limited repertoire of strategies to draw upon when reading. They are often afraid of books and resist reading, which is no surprise as they struggle through texts, not making much sense of them and relying almost exclusively on phonetic decoding (an approach to reading instruction that many of them have been immersed in since they were kindergartners). These students generally resist reading shorter or less complex texts that may be more accessible and comprehensible to them for fear that they will be teased by their peers for reading "baby books." They generally do poorly on standardized tests and are labelled as "poor readers" or "below grade-level readers." When faced with such struggling readers, many upper-grade teachers do not know how to attend to their students' needs. In some cases, they are accustomed to having students who are already readers. In other cases, they have had more experience with less experienced readers. However, regardless of their circumstances, these teachers often have one thing in common—they aren't sure how to effectively teach beginning reading strategies to older, emerging readers. Many upper-grade teachers, including Gail, have addressed this dilemma in one or more of the following ways: a) sending students to a lower grade classroom for reading instruction, b) placing students in an obviously low-level reading group within the classroom, c) sending students out to a special remedial reading program, or d) bringing in a tutor. All of these methods, however, focus on students' weaknesses and inadequacies. While they may be viable alternatives in many situations, each can have a negative impact on students' self-esteem.

For years, Gail has been frustrated by not knowing how to reach her struggling readers. Many of them felt stigmatized and self-conscious when tutors came to help them with their reading, and they often refused the help. Several years ago, Gail moved away from skills-based reading textbooks to a literature-based program, at the center of which is literature study circles (see Eeds & Wells 1989; Peterson & Eeds 1990; Samway et al. 1991). In literature study circles, all of the students, including the least fluent readers, have choices about which books they will read. They then join discussion circles made up of students and the teacher who have all read the same book. Although the least successful readers enthusiastically participate in these discussions, Gail sees how they have access to only a limited number of reading strategies, which often influences how much they understand.

Buddy reading has helped, however, by providing a powerful and non-threatening way to teach reading strategies to these older students. In minilessons that are designed to prepare them for teaching the younger students, we have explored many reading strategies, including how the purpose of reading is to make meaning (as opposed to decoding perfectly, word by word), and strategies for creating meaning (e.g., using illustrations to get clues and using context to make predictions). We share these reading strategies with the older students for use in their teaching role, but they then become accessible to them as readers. These are strategies that many of the students did not use in the past, and they are strategies that we now observe them using as readers. Choulaphone wrote about how she is able to use a strategy that she learned in buddy reading when reading other books that do not have pictures: "The book that don't have picture I just think what happen in my mind whiled Im reading." Tamara also described how buddy reading has influenced what she does when she comes upon a word she doesn't know: "I skip that word and then I read the words around that word. I could also sound out the word so I could know how to say it. But I think I could brake up the words. Like Mississipps. Miss-i-ss-i-pp-i = Mississippi, Or comment, com-ment = comment."

When Kim Lon, a fifth-grade girl, entered the class midyear, it was clear that she had a hard time understanding much of what she read. Her comments to us support the notion that buddy reading has helped her become a more successful and skilled reader, as the following journal entry illustrates. In this case, she has learned how asking herself questions has helped her become a more independent reader:

> What really helped me in my own reading from buddy reading is when I reminds my self about which more question that I have to ask myself like I was asking my buddy and start a conversation.
> So then I will start my own conversation myself and ask my self.
> That's how buddy reading helps me and I like that.

This year Kim Lon has become a reader. Although she still has some trouble with comprehension, she actively participates in literature study circles, asks questions when she doesn't understand, and loves to read.

As everyone is reading picture books in preparation for buddy reading, there is no stigma attached to reading these so-called "baby books." In fact, many of the older students have commented on how much they have enjoyed reading picture books and how they have experienced success as readers. Paul wrote, "It has helped me fined better books to read. Also in reading I can finsh them in time." Josh commented, "Buddy reading has helped me by giving me practice at reading I never would have gotten if it wouldn't have been for buddy reading." Students such as Josh are frequently daunted by the length of books they encounter in the upper grades and, because of their lack of experience as readers, tend to resist reading . . . and rarely read an entire book. Reading for the buddy reading sessions allows these students to experience the satisfaction of being able to read entire books in a short amount of time.

Students' comments such as these show us how the buddy reading program can serve as an effective way to teach reading strategies to older elementary students. Now, when Gail sees that students are still emergent readers, she knows that she will probably be able to address some of their needs through buddy reading minilessons, in addition to the support that she provides in the fifth-/sixth-grade language arts program. Through working with their younger buddies, the students get practice in using strategies that are often helpful to them also.

## USING OBSERVATIONS OF STUDENTS TO INFORM INSTRUCTIONAL DECISIONS

The importance of taking time to observe the students and taking anecdotal records is one powerful effect that the buddy reading program has had on Mary and Gail. From listening to the students and discussing field notes with Katharine and Jenny, they came to see the tremendous benefits of carefully observing students, and both have now developed a system to help them do this.

Both teachers had been aware of the importance of keeping anecdotal records for several years. At the beginning of each year, they would start to organize their note-taking systems. By mid-semester, however, they were rarely entering any observations. They tried various systems (e.g., stick-on address labels, notebooks, and three-by-five index cards), but still their efforts petered out rather quickly. They now think that this may have been because they did not really understand how it could help them as teachers. It wasn't until Katharine and Jenny came into their classrooms and shared observations with them that Mary and Gail realized what they had been missing. The field notes provided concrete data on students' language and literacy development and social skills. For example, Mary found out that Monica was able to write and was, in fact, acting as a resource to her peers. She heard how Darron was using strategies that she had first taught earlier in the year: if you need help spelling a word, try to sound it out or try to find it somewhere in the room. Up to this point, Mary had been unaware that Darron was using these strategies. Gail heard how María was a fluent reader in Spanish who used her knowledge of print when reading books in English with her buddy. She also learned how Antoine, a boy who was often uncooperative, kept detailed and perceptive field notes one day when his buddy was absent, despite the fact that he had been furious at not having a partner. They began to see what students could do.

This kind of information excited Mary and Gail, but they were still initially resistant to taking on the role of observer, in addition to teacher and manager. Katharine had been encouraging them to keep track of their observations for quite a while, pointing out the positive effects this could have on their students' growth and their lives as teachers. But Mary and Gail questioned the feasibility of doing this in a class of thirty students, thinking that Katharine was suggesting that they keep the detailed kinds of observations that she recorded. Eventually they realized that they could spend a few minutes at a time carefully observing and recording what they heard students say or what they saw them do.

The next step was to find a manageable system for gathering and storing these anecdotal records. In the past, this type of note-taking had often seemed laborious, cumbersome, and just one more task to do in a very busy day. Mary would leave index cards strewn around the room. Post-its that she had carefully stuck to pages in a notebook would become unstuck and flutter to the floor. Gail would write random notes on scraps of paper or in her planning book, but they too often got misplaced or put aside. The note-taking didn't yet seem to be having much of an impact on their teaching. It didn't really have a focus then. This has changed, however, since they have begun to use their detailed observations to inform them as teachers. Now they also have record-keeping systems that work for them. Mary keeps notes on each student on five-by-eight inch index cards that are taped one on top of the other like a flip chart. These cards are stored in a daily observations folder that is made from a manila file folder (see Figure 13). The children's names are printed on the bottom of each card so that she can easily find a child's card. Once a card is filled with notes, Mary places it in the child's long-term folder, and replaces it in the daily record folder with another five-by-eight card. Gail carries a legal-size manila folder that is divided into thirty-six spaces, each containing a post-it for each child (see Figure 14). A child's name is written on the top of each box. At the end of the buddy reading session, she transfers completed post-its to those individual students' pages in a large binder. In this way, both teachers have on-going, dated records on each student. We also use photographs to document student achievement and progress. For instance, a photograph of an older student sitting close to a younger buddy, both of them comfortably holding the book, the younger child listening attentively as the older student tracks the print with a pointed finger, is a very evocative record of the older student using bedtime reading strategies quite effectively (see Photo 18).

Realizing that it is impossible to carefully observe thirty students in a half-hour buddy reading session, we have found that it is more

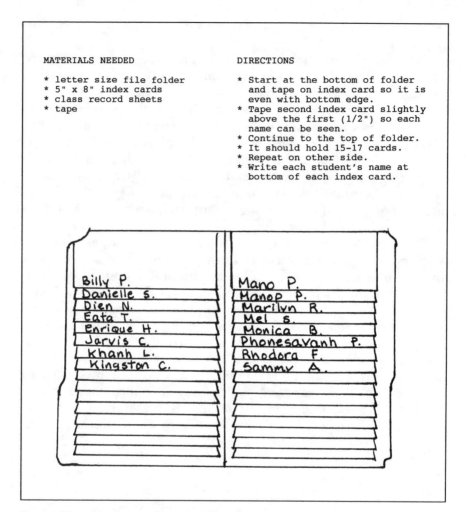

MATERIALS NEEDED

* letter size file folder
* 5" x 8" index cards
* class record sheets
* tape

DIRECTIONS

* Start at the bottom of folder and tape on index card so it is even with bottom edge.
* Tape second index card slightly above the first (1/2") so each name can be seen.
* Continue to the top of folder.
* It should hold 15-17 cards.
* Repeat on other side.
* Write each student's name at bottom of each index card.

Billy P.
Danielle S.
Dien N.
Eata T.
Enrique H.
Jarvis C.
Khanh L.
Kingston C.

Mano P.
Manop P.
Marilyn R.
Mel S.
Monica B.
Phonesavanh P.
Rhodora F.
Sammy A.

FIGURE 13    *Mary's record-keeping system.*

effective for the two teachers to focus on two to three pairs of students in each classroom each week. In this way, they can both move around the room to check in with several students while also engaging in lengthier, more detailed observations of a few students. A short three- to five-minute observation can provide a wealth of information about: a) how students interact socially and academically, b) the learning and teaching strategies that students use, and c) how children interact and perform in different situations.

The teachers use their notes as the basis for lunchtime meetings that follow the buddy reading session. They share observations, briefly discuss concerns and problems, and plan for the next week's session. These written observations and discussions have helped each of us become better observers of students and teachers. We have

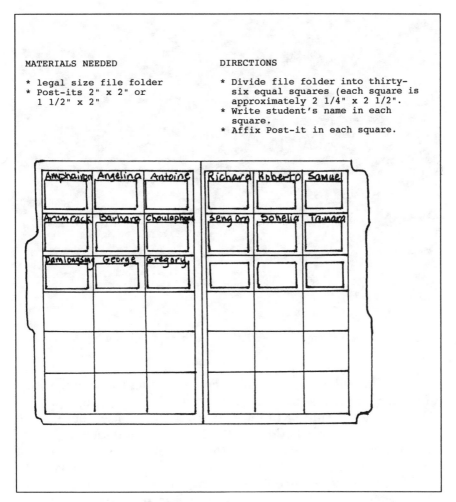

MATERIALS NEEDED

* legal size file folder
* Post-its 2" x 2" or
  1 1/2" x 2"

DIRECTIONS

* Divide file folder into thirty-
  six equal squares (each square is
  approximately 2 1/4" x 2 1/2".
* Write student's name in each
  square.
* Affix Post-it in each square.

| Amphaivon | Angelina | Antoine | | Richard | Roberto | Samuel |
| Arumrack | Barbara | Choulophoa | | Seng Orn | Sohelia | Tamara |
| Damloagsma | George | Gregory | | | | |

FIGURE 14    *Gail's record-keeping system.*

learned how powerful anecdotal notetaking can be for assessing students' strengths and needs. For example, notes have allowed us to see how Richard has progressed from being very focused on his own needs as a reader during buddy reading (e.g., holding the book very close to him so that he could concentrate on reading aloud, but making it difficult for his buddy to see the pages), to being very critical of his buddy's emerging reading strategies (e.g., chastising him for not reading all the words on the page), to being a very supportive listener (e.g., being totally engrossed during the reading and congratulating his buddy on doing such a good job).

The notes have also helped us to see that José had a long-term problem with an uncooperative buddy, which inspired us to carefully observe the pair, and talk with him in depth to understand his perceptions of the situation. Particularly at the beginning of the year,

Photo 18   *Photo record of an older student using bedtime reading strategies.*

many of the older students comment on inattentive buddies, so it would have been easy to ignore José's quandary, thinking that it was simply a normal kind of problem that would sort itself out in time, once José had learned additional teaching and interactional strategies. The notes reminded us that José's situation was potentially different. It was, and we changed partners, and both students had a very successful experience for the remainder of the year.

Observational note-taking helped us realize one day recently that Gail and Mary were observing only half of their respective classes. We realized that we needed to make a change so that they would be able to observe all their students during buddy reading. One option is to switch groups of children every two months. In this way, they will be able to observe all their students during buddy reading over the course of the school year.

## USING STUDENT FEEDBACK TO ENHANCE OUR TEACHING

Debriefing sessions and reflective journals are two of the ways we receive feedback on what is occurring during the buddy reading sessions. During their weekly planning meetings, Mary and Gail try to read through the children's journal entries, noting concerns and insights the students raise. Barbara recently wrote in her journal about her buddy, Manop, "Well buddy reading today whent great he was really reading the book everey time I pointed to the thing that it said in the book he will read it he felt very proud of himself." When Mary read Barbara's journal, she was amazed and said, "I had no idea that Manop could read so well independently. I never saw him exhibit this type of literate behavior before." When with her, Manop had very little confidence in his ability to read independently. After reading Barbara's entry, she re-evaluated her approach with Manop. She learned that he seemed to read more fluently and take more risks with other children. Therefore, she decided to pair him up with a second grade peer buddy.

In the beginning, we found that we were almost exclusively observing the buddy pairs that might present a problem due to lack of fluency in a shared language, behavior, or reading experience. Because we felt we were observing all pairs equally, we were startled to read Tamara's journal entry in which she chastised Gail for spending too much time with a few students: ". . . I think Ms. Whang is always with Jesús or Paul. But never with anyone else. Others need help also. So I hope she does." We learned several lessons from Tamara. She was right. Our observations focused on the same few students and we were paying more attention to the boys. This is especially upsetting to us as we prided ourselves on fostering a democratic classroom atmosphere that was free of gender bias. We realized that we could not ignore a buddy pair that was working without apparent incident. Apart from the fact that we would learn a lot about them and about successful cross-age tutoring strategies from observing such pairs, we couldn't assume that they didn't need or want help and encouragement. This was a very sobering experience for us.

We realized that Tamara's journal entry was a criticism of her teacher, but this encouraged us as Gail had been working hard to create a classroom environment in which students could feel confident about taking risks, and Tamara had clearly and effectively done this. The entry also served as a warning to us that we needed to be more consistent about reading the journals as they could reveal a great deal that we needed to be aware of. Sometimes we didn't read them for several weeks at a time, and Tamara's accurate assessment revealed a situation that needed to be addressed immediately. Since then we have been trying to read journals on a weekly basis. It is sometimes hard to find the time in a busy day, but it is worth it.

We have learned how important debriefing sessions are to us as teachers. In addition to learning more about the students, as individuals and as cohort groups, the content of these sessions has frequently influenced the focus of subsequent minilessons. That is, instead of curricular guides telling us what to teach, we follow the lead of the students and teach skills and strategies that they indicate a need for. In the debriefing sessions we have been alerted to issues that continue to be a problem, even after being addressed before, e.g., careful book selection and discussion strategies. For example, at the beginning of the year, the older buddies would complain about the books that the younger children were bringing to the buddy reading sessions. Damlongsong said, "I had to do all the reading cause he couldn't read any books. Ms. Whang, I thought you said they had to read, too?" These comments prompted Mary to talk with her class about successful book selection strategies.

Other students complained that their buddies were bringing the same books every week and that it was boring for them. Gail realized that she needed to talk with them again about how beginning readers bring the same books to buddy reading because they can read them and therefore feel successful; she addressed the issue the next week before buddy reading. During another debriefing session, Paul complained that his buddy didn't talk, only saying, "Yes, No, or I don't know." Several other children agreed with him that this was a problem. From this feedback, Gail realized that many of the children needed help in developing a range of discussion strategies, which she reviewed in the next minilesson.

One day in Mary's class, as the children were debriefing, Sounthavy complained, "The book was too long. It was boring." Billy echoed him, "Yeah, long books are boring." The discussion that followed prompted Mary to reorganize her classroom library, and she added a section for easy-to-read books. She also spent time during the following week teaching the children strategies for: a) choosing books that they could read to their older buddies, and b) finding interesting books for the older buddies to read to them.

Sometimes, the feedback we get needs or merits an immediate response (e.g., when there is a crisis brewing or when the issue affects only one student). This is when we take advantage of the "teachable moment." However, many, many issues are raised in debriefing sessions, and we have learned to keep track of them and then address some of the more common issues in a minilesson before the next buddy reading session. In this way, they can be attended to in greater depth. Also, teaching strategies right before a buddy reading session seems to encourage the students to pay more attention to what they are doing and try strategies that they might not be familiar with.

## COLLABORATIVE REFLECTION INFLUENCING THE DEVELOPMENT OF OUR CURRICULA

Teachers do not often make or take the time to reflect on their teaching or collaborate with other teachers, and this is understandable given the enormous demands placed upon us. However, we cannot stress how valuable and exciting it has been to collaborate and reflect together. When Gail and Mary began buddy reading six years ago, they would meet together for ten minutes or so on an irregular and unpredictable basis. They now meet regularly, often over lunch, to discuss what they have observed during each buddy reading session. They sometimes talk on the phone or meet briefly after school to reflect on the previous session and plan for the next one. At other times they meet in the evening. These meetings lead to greater insights into students, generate concrete ideas for the next week's minilessons, and allow them to raise and attend to concerns and problems that they need to address.

Collaboration is rare between primary and intermediate teachers (and between elementary and university teachers). For years Mary and Gail knew that they shared similar ideas about education, but they never collaborated in any in-depth way. Even when they first began the buddy reading program, they prepared their classes for the tutoring sessions independently, with very little communication between them. In the past few years, however, since we all began collaborating, we have seen that we can learn a lot from each other. For example, Gail has learned a great deal about emerging reading and writing processes and strategies, and has been able to access this new-found knowledge when working with her least successful and experienced readers and writers. It was during a meeting with Mary and Katharine that Gail learned about the role that phonics plays for emergent readers in a learner-centered language arts program. This topic had been prompted by Paul coming up to Gail one day and saying very matter-of-factly that his buddy, Kingston, didn't know the sounds of the letters T, R, and K. He had made this diagnosis when reading a book with Kingston. Gail was excited about Paul being so observant and borrowed K, R, and T letter books from Mary for Paul to use as a resource. During the following week's buddy reading session, Gail noticed that Paul was asking Kingston to sound out every letter in every word that he did not know how to read, e.g., "appreciate" and "unfortunately." They were reading *The Elephant and the Bad Baby* (Vipont 1986), and at the beginning, Kingston tried to comply. Later on, though, he became restless:

PAUL: What sound does this make? [Pointing to *g* in *gingersnaps.*]
KINGSTON: Guh.
PAUL: Good job. Now what sound does this make? [Pointing to the *i.*]
KINGSTON: Ih.
PAUL: What does this say? [Pointing to the *n.*]
KINGSTON: Nnnn. I'm tired. I don't want to read no more.
PAUL: But we're not finished the book. You're suppose to read the book.
KINGSTON: I've got a stomachache. [He puts his head down on the desk.]

After observing the pair for a few minutes, Gail began to question this use of phonics in reading, and suggested to Paul that he finish reading the book to Kingston. What had usually been a pleasant session had become a massive struggle between Paul and Kingston, with Paul repeatedly admonishing Kingston to pay attention.

As Gail observed this faltering interaction, she wondered about her role in encouraging Paul to use phonics in this way. When we met later, Gail shared her observations and concerns, which led to a discussion about when and where to use phonics. It became apparent that Gail herself was unclear about the use of phonics in the reading process. We spent a lot of time discussing a range of emerging reading strategies, including phonics, and decided that the "sounding out" process that Gail had taught in a minilesson might be more appropriately used when students were writing. She decided that she needed to share her misgivings about over-using "sounding out" as a reading strategy with her students and make sure that they were familiar and comfortable with other reading strategies, e.g., using picture and context clues.

At another meeting, when we were talking about the rich insights that the older students had during a debriefing session, Mary realized that this was an area which she had neglected in her own classroom. She had seen the benefits of the debriefing session that followed each week's buddy reading session for the older students, but wasn't convinced that debriefing sessions could work with younger children. We discussed why younger children should be given opportunities to reflect in this way (e.g., we needed to know how the younger children felt about the sessions—what were they learning; what concerns did they have. If they were expected to reflect upon the experience, perhaps they would be more invested in it.). Eventually, Mary introduced the class to debriefing sessions. At first, she was rather disappointed because the children seemed to repeat the same refrains, e.g., "Buddy reading is fun," "I like my buddy," "My buddy is nice." This was disappointing to her because she was not receiving the same kind of rich and varied feedback that Gail heard. The children were not bringing up concerns or problems. We wondered if it had become something of a meaningless, routinized event. Then one day there wasn't a debriefing session because of other demands on the day. As the children lined up to go to lunch, they called out in dismay, "But our debriefing, we didn't debrief!" "We need to debrief before we go to lunch." This was a surprising but reassuring response, and Mary saw that it was an important aspect of the program for the students. Although many of the younger students were not as verbal as the older students, we discovered that they were just as aware of what was happening in their pairs and had specific ideas and concerns.

Another positive outcome of the buddy reading program was that both teachers began to notice the learning of all the students, not just those students in their respective classes. Mary noticed the growth of Vanessa as she began to focus less on herself and more on the needs of her younger buddy, Danielle. She also observed how excited Vanessa became as Danielle began to respond to Vanessa's attention. Gail noticed how Malcolm beamed with pride as his buddy, Jesús, encouraged him to continue with his picture reading; she began to follow Malcolm's development as a reader. Instead of just one teacher noticing students' accomplishments, struggles, and needs, now there are at least two. As a consequence of these collaborative efforts, we are better able to understand students' learning processes, and plan effective and appropriate teaching strategies.

## THE IMPORTANCE OF CONDUCTING RESEARCH IN THE CLASSROOM

During their discussions, Gail, Mary and Katharine have raised many questions that they would like to explore in more depth. These questions are grounded in what they see during the buddy reading sessions, questions the students raise, and questions they have regarding more effective ways of teaching and learning. Teachers rarely have time to consciously look for solutions to their questions and do this kind of research in their classes. One issue that interested us all is grounded in discussion patterns. We had noticed how discussions seemed to fall apart after students had read books together: the younger children were often reluctant to talk, and the older students sometimes resorted to a stream of closed questions (e.g., Did you like this book? What's this?). Also, we had seen how both groups of students were not always effective during literature study discussions (in the upper-grade classroom) and book discussions (in the lower-grade classroom). We decided to investigate what we could do to help students facilitate discussions among themselves. In order to explore this question, we observed students reading and discussing books, conducted minilessons, kept anecdotal notes recording exact conversations, and consulted with individual students. This allowed us to see how the children were thinking, evaluate the effectiveness of the minilessons taught each week, and make sure that future instructional opportunities would be relevant and in tune with students' needs. For example, when Soheila said in a debriefing session that she was frustrated because she could not get a discussion going, we asked her to role-play with Gail the frustrating situation she was having with her buddy, Yien Fou, a very shy and quiet child. Through this minilesson, Soheila and the other students learned more strategies for getting a discussion started (e.g., sharing what we think about a book, making connections to our own lives).

After exploring this issue for four weeks, the older class had access to several helpful discussion strategies, many of which came from the students themselves. Damlongsong shared a strategy he found helpful, "I try to ask a funny question like 'Do you want to eat catsup with your grass?' or 'Would you like the Troll to drown in milk?'" Using her anecdotal notes, Gail shared a strategy that Magali used with her buddy:

> Magali asked her buddy questions about the story before reading it. She also tried to connect the story to Khanh's life with the question, "Do you have a brother who eats a lot?" She also shared her own experience about her brother. Finally she made Khanh the expert about snow which got Khanh talking. Because she had never seen snow, Magali asked Khanh to tell her about it.

Mary conducted a minilesson where she modeled both unsuccessful and successful discussions with an older buddy. She played the part of the younger buddy who simply shrugged her shoulders and said, "I don't know," in response to questions about a book. The younger children saw the frustration that the older children experience when their buddies don't engage in a discussion of the book. She contrasted this with another role-play in which both participants were involved. These strategies have apparently had a positive impact on discussions during buddy reading as we rarely hear complaints about ineffective or boring discussions.

## PHYSICAL ORGANIZATION OF THE CLASSROOM

Buddy reading has caused us to rethink the physical organization of the classrooms. We have reorganized them so that student pairs have quiet areas in which to meet, rather than all gathering in the same general space. For example, in the first/second-grade classroom there is a library corner with rocking chairs, a few pillows, and a large beanbag chair. In another corner there is a large multicolored striped rug where the class meets for discussions, debriefing sessions, and minilessons. Another area has rectangular tables that each seat six children. As the students enter the classrooms, many of the buddy pairs go immediately to a favorite spot. Sid can be found sprawling on the large beanbag chair with his buddy, Angela, sitting cross-legged beside him. Marilyn always heads for the rocking chair with her buddy close behind her. Eata and Tamara prefer to sit in chairs at a table by the window. Other pairs may pick a different spot each week. The pairs find their self-chosen spots and begin their reading, almost before the last pair is seated. Some children also work well sitting outside or in the hallway. In these cases, they take chairs with them. What we have found is that it is important for the buddies to have the quiet and privacy they need to effectively inter-act. At the same time, many of them benefit from being in close proximity to each other so they can listen to and learn from each other. This means that a flexible classroom setup is essential.

The buddy reading program has also prompted us to organize the classroom libraries so that students can more easily locate books that they wish to share together. For example, in the past the first/second-grade library had only a few categories (e.g., storybooks, ani-mal books, poems and songs, ABC books, and theme books) and most of the books were stored in bookcases. As we began to expect the younger students to take more responsibility for good book selections, we realized that the classroom libraries needed to be reor-ganized and books made more accessible to the children. Now we use both shelves and crates to store books as the children can more easily see what is available (see Photo 19). We store the books according to the following categories:

- Animal stories
- ABC books
- Easy storybooks
- Dinosaur books
- Poetry
- Nonfiction
- Partner reading (two copies so two students can read together)
- Fairy tales/Folk tales
- Storybooks/Fiction
- Holiday books
- Biography
- Sunshine Books (a series of predictable books)
- Wonder World (a series of predictable books)
- Twig Books (a series of predictable books)
- I Want to Know About (a series of nonfiction books)
- Let's Read and Find Out Science Books (a series of nonfiction books)
- Big Books (large print books)
- Beginner Books (a series of books)
- I Can Read Books (a series of books)
- Nonfiction magazines (e.g., *Nature, Ranger Rick, My Big Backyard*)

Each section is color coded with stick-on dots (e.g., a red dot indi-cates a storybook, while an orange dot is an easy-to-read book) This allows the children to more easily find books that they are able to read and that are of interest to them.

PHOTO 19   *Organizing books.*

## EXTENDING OUR WORK BEYOND OUR CLASSROOMS

As Gail and Mary sit in the teachers' lunchroom each week discussing that day's buddy reading session, other teachers can't help but over-hear the excitement in their voices, and that excitement is contagious. Buddy reading programs are springing up throughout the school and teachers are seeking out colleagues in hopes of starting their own program. This year, twelve classrooms are involved in a buddy reading program. In order to ensure the success of these new programs, Gail and Mary have begun a support group that meets monthly. In the past, some of these same teachers attempted buddy reading pro-grams, but abandoned them when problems arose. During the meet-ings, questions arise, solutions to problems are brainstormed, and successes are shared. During the first session, the group discussed a draft of Chapter Two of this book, "Initial Preparation for a Buddy Reading Program," as several of the teachers wanted to explore how to set up a program.

Until relatively recently, both Mary and Gail's teaching interests and concerns were limited to their immediate grade levels. More recently, however, they have both found that their interests have broadened to include both younger and older learners. For exam-ple, Mary used to regard herself as strictly a primary teacher, and focused almost exclusively on the skills and curricula that relate most directly to the early grades. Whenever the upper-grade teachers discussed a program they were implementing, she tended not to pay attention as she was not particularly interested in issues relating to the upper grades. She felt that there was only so much information she could focus on at any given time.

In the past couple of years, however, since working closely with Gail in improving the buddy reading program, she has begun to become more interested and involved in the education of all the students at Hawthorne School. She is now interested in issues that most directly effect other grades, including a kindergarten through fourth grade portfolio assessment project. As part of this project, she now helps to conduct monthly workshops for teachers of all grades.

Another area in which the buddy reading program has been extended is in having college students become pen-pals to the buddy pairs. Gail is co-teaching a credential program social studies methods class at a local college, and has partnered each college student with a buddy pair. The college students correspond with both a first/second and fifth/sixth grader in order to become more aware of the writing and thinking abilities of elementary students. The elementary students have an authentic opportunity to write to others.

The buddy reading experience has had a profound impact on Katharine, also. While working with Gail and Mary, she has been a full-time professor at a local university where she is a teacher educator. The weekly visits to their classrooms to collect data and the frequent meetings we have throughout the week to discuss what we observed and plan for future sessions, have kept her grounded in elementary classrooms. It has not only provided her with current examples and experiences to share with her own students, who are either practicing or prospective teachers, but it has enhanced her understanding of children's learning processes. Corresponding with Gail in letters and notes has helped to clarify her thinking, as have the weekly meetings with both teachers. For example, she is particularly concerned about the older, least experienced readers who generally struggle throughout their school experience. She has noticed how their need for instruction in reading strategies is either misplaced or misdirected (e.g., in programs where the focus is on skills, drills, and worksheets) or virtually nonexistent (e.g., in classrooms where teachers have thrown out the baby with the bath water, focusing exclusively on "just reading"). Working with Gail and Mary has helped her to better figure out the kinds of strategy lessons that many of these older readers could benefit from, e.g., asking readers if what they just read makes sense, asking about the reading strategies the student uses when faced with an unfamiliar text, predicting what the unfamiliar word is likely to be, given the context.

## THE INFLUENCE OF WRITING
## THIS BOOK ON US AS TEACHERS

Another way in which we have been changed as teachers is intimately connected to this book. We have spent many hours working both separately and together writing the book, trying to provide an accurate and evocative picture of our buddy reading program; we hope that readers catch at least a glimpse of the excitement that this experience has engendered in both the students and us. Even as we write this book, we are changing as teachers. The act of reflection is a profound catalyst for change. We find that we are constantly stopping to reconsider our practices, what we do as teachers and why we do what we do. For example, while working on the section in which we discuss the pairing of students (Chapter Two), we found ourselves clarifying what exactly influenced our decisions. We have friends and colleagues who leave the composition of small groups or pairs to chance and we asked ourselves why we didn't do the same. Our conversation helped us to see that, in fact, many of the buddy pairings are actually quite random. However, there have been several cases in which the special needs of students have been pronounced and we have had to attend to those needs, usually by taking into consideration the particular strengths and skills of those same students or other students. One example of this is the pairing of Khouanchith with Angelina. Khouanchith is an easily distractible child who has a difficult time sitting still for more than five minutes. He wanders around the classroom or rolls around on the rug. Mary felt that he needed a firm but warm and supportive older buddy with whom to work. Angelina is such a student and we have seen Khouanchith settle down and begin to focus more.

Working together in this way inevitably means clarifying thoughts, figuring out whether we agree with each other, making compromises, and revising accordingly. In this way, we came to understand why the younger children were only reflecting upon their buddy reading experiences orally. In an earlier draft, Mary had explained that she did it this way for several reasons, including the following:

- many of the children are unable to write more than one or two words
- many of the children are not very familiar with developmental (invented) spelling strategies
- children need lots of practice talking about the buddy reading experience before being asked to write their reflections.

As Katharine read this section, it didn't make sense to her. For example, she knew that written reflections didn't have to be written in conventional spelling—in fact, she knew that Mary encouraged her students to draw their thoughts and write as best they could . . . and they did so in writers' workshop. In the process of discussing this section, Mary was eventually able to put her finger on what was troubling her. She realized that she had been intimidated by the fluency and thoughtfulness of the older students' written reflections and was comparing what her students did with what students who were four to six years older were doing. Once she recognized this, she was able to move forward as a teacher and invited her class to also reflect upon the buddy reading sessions in print.

## WHAT NOW?

We have learned from and been changed in dramatic ways by this odyssey called buddy reading. Our learning seems to be constant. Never ending. And that's one of the most exciting aspects of the program for us. Although we know that the program is solid and running effectively, we see elements that we need to improve upon, some of which follow.

We need to have a greater selection of multicultural picture books which reflect the diversity of the students at Hawthorne School. Gail's fifth/sixth-grade reading program is grounded in literature study circles, and she now has an extensive collection of novels that are written by African Americans, Asian Americans, and Latinos (e.g., Candy Dawson Boyd, who is African American and Gary Soto who is Latino), and/or portray the lives and experiences of these groups in non-stereotypical ways (e.g., *Children of the River* [Crew 1989], which is about a Cambodian girl who fled from her country in a boat and now lives in Oregon). However, few of the picture books that the children read together (particularly the predictable books that are so successful with emerging readers) are as representative of the diverse cultural and linguistic groups that are present in the classrooms, school, and neighborhood. We have discovered that this is a reflection of what is currently available in print—we hope that publishers will remedy this void in children's literature. There are, though, books that Gail and Mary can add to their class libraries, and they are using their book allocations to enhance their collections with more multicultural and bilingual picture books. We also borrow books from friends, colleagues, and libraries, and are writing small grants.

We need to have a broader selection of nonfiction. We have discovered that some of the children are much more interested in nonfiction—children's nature magazines have been particularly popular. However, at the moment the majority of books in the two classrooms is fiction. We realize that we need to augment the book collections in each classroom with more nonfiction books and magazines. We are on the lookout for easy-to-read nonfiction books for each of the classrooms. Information books written by the older students have helped to fill the void.

We need to provide opportunities for the older students to observe each other on occasion so as to learn from each other. At the moment, the only time that the older students have opportunities to do this is when there is an uneven number of students. When students have observed each other and kept field notes they have learned a lot, just as teachers do when we have opportunities to observe each other.

We need to organize a support group for Hawthorne teachers who are interested in a cross-age reading program. One day, another teacher met Gail in the hallway and said, "I really need to talk. When are you meeting next? My kids hate buddy reading." It turned out that six of his students did not enjoy the experience, so Gail suggested that he ask them why. We have found that students' responses to the program are directly related to the degree to which the program is owned by them; this means that teachers have to listen to students and respond to their comments, suggestions, and needs. We believe that teachers need support from each other if we are to succeed in implementing student-centered learning environments, and a buddy reading support group is just one possibility.

We need to work closely with the older students who enter the upper-grade class in the middle of the year. Although we have seen how the class benefits a great deal from the month-long preparation that is held at the beginning of the year, we had not been providing a similar introduction to the program for students who transferred into the school after the beginning of the year, and we have seen how some of the students have struggled. In order to help newcomers have a more successful experience, we will be implementing the following strategies in the future:

1. Provide a training period in which the new student is paired with an older buddy.
2. Meet with the student in a small group to explain and discuss the program.
3. Lead a minilesson in which other students offer tips for the new tutor.
4. Provide opportunities for the newcomer to observe successful buddy pairs, and suggest a focus for the observations (e.g., How did the tutors get the discussion off the ground? or What kinds of questions did the tutors ask?).
5. Pay special attention to the pairing and try to ensure a successful match.
6. When the buddy pair meets for the first time, focus on an inclusion activity (e.g., cooking together, or meet first with a list of questions to find the answers to).

We need to build upon the cultural and linguistic diversity that is present in the two classrooms. Both Mary and Gail place a great deal of emphasis on the benefits of living in a multilingual, multicultural world, and many of the learning events that students engage in throughout the year underscore this. This is true for buddy reading also, for example, when the students cook together or participate in art and craft projects. We also encourage students to talk with each other about customs and traditions they engage in at home, both day-to-day practices and special events, such as holidays. We encourage them to use their native languages whenever possible, and share their respective languages, when they do not have a common native language. However, we realize that we should be placing more of an emphasis on this critical element during buddy reading. We have already discussed our efforts to locate more multicultural and bilingual books and magazines. In addition, we have been seeking out books written in the native languages of the students.

As we reflect upon the effects that this program has had upon our teaching and beyond, we realize that the effects are ongoing. We will continue to explore issues and questions within elementary classrooms. We will continue to collaborate as it has become a part of our lives. The community of learners that we try to establish in our respective classrooms extends to other communities of learners that include our colleagues. Through the process of writing this book, we have explored many issues, many new to us, and this is deepening our understanding of what it means to be a teacher in the twenty-first century.

# Appendix: Popular Books and Magazines for Buddy Reading

## PATTERNED LANGUAGE BOOKS: SHORTER AND WORDLESS TEXTS

Asbjornsen, P.C. and J.E. Moe. 1957. *The Three Billy Goats Gruff*. New York: Harcourt, Brace & World Inc.

Asch, Frank. 1984. *Just Like Daddy*. Englewood Cliffs, NJ: Prentice-Hall.

Bang, Molly. 1983. *Ten Nine Eight*. New York: Greenwillow Books.

Barchas, Sarah E. 1983. *I Was Walking Down the Road*. New York: Scholastic.

Bayer, Jane. 1984. *A My Name is Alice*. New York: Dial.

Becker, John. 1983. *Seven Little Rabbits*. New York: Scholastic.

Berenstain, Stanley, and Janice Berenstain. 1971. *The B Book*. New York: Random House.

Brown, Margaret Wise. 1977. *The Runaway Bunny*. New York: Harper & Row.

Brown, Ruth. 1984. *A Dark, Dark Tale*. New York: Dial.

Browne, Anthony. 1987. *I Like Books*. New York: Knopf.

———. 1989. *Things I Like*. New York: Knopf.

Carle, Eric. 1975. *The Mixed Up Chameleon*. New York: Thomas Y. Crowell.

———. 1981. *The Very Hungry Caterpillar*. New York: Putnam.

———. 1984. *The Grouchy Ladybug*. New York: Thomas Y. Crowell.

———. 1986. *The Very Busy Spider*. New York: Scholastic.

———. 1989. *The Tiny Seed*. New York: Scholastic.

Carlson, Nancy. 1988. *I Like Me!* New York: Penguin Books.

Carlstrom, Nancy. 1986. *Jesse Bear, What Will You Wear?* New York: Macmillan.

Christelow, Eileen. 1991. *Five Little Monkeys Sitting in a Tree*. New York: The Trumpet Club.

Cowley, Joy. 1987a. *The Birthday Cake*. San Diego: The Wright Group.

———. 1987b. *Huggles' Breakfast*. San Diego: The Wright Group.

———. 1987c. *Just This Once*. San Diego: The Wright Group.

———. 1987d. *Meanies*. San Diego: The Wright Group.

———. 1987e. *Mrs. Wishy-Washy*. San Diego: The Wright Group.

———. 1987f. *The Poor Sore Paw*. San Diego: The Wright Group.

———. 1987g. *Yuck Soup*. San Diego: The Wright Group.

Crews, Donald. 1987. *School Bus*. New York: Penguin Books (Puffin Books).

———. 1978. *Freight Train*. New York: Greenwillow Books.

Galdone, Paul. 1973a. *The Little Red Hen*. New York: Scholastic Inc.

———. 1973b. *The Three Bears*. New York: Clarion Books.

———. 1975. *The Gingerbread Boy*. New York: Clarion Books.

———— . 1981. *The Three Billy Goats Gruff.* Boston: Houghton Mifflin.

———— . 1984. *The Three Little Pigs.* Boston: Houghton Mifflin.

Gelman, Rita. 1977. *Why Can't I Fly?* New York: Scholastic.

———— . 1987. *More Spaghetti I Say.* New York: Scholastic.

Ginsburg, Mirra. 1980. *Good Morning Chick.* New York: Scholastic.

Hutchins, Pat. 1968. *Rosie's Walk.* New York: Macmillan.

———— . 1972. *Good-Night Owl.* New York: Macmillan.

———— . 1987. *The Doorbell Rang.* New York: Scholastic.

Johnson, Crockett. 1969. *Harold and the Purple Crayon.* New York: Harper & Row.

Kalan, Robert. 1978. *Rain.* New York: Greenwillow Books.

———— . 1979. *Blue Sea.* New York: Greenwillow Books.

———— . 1981. *Jump, Frog, Jump!* New York: Greenwillow Books.

Keats, Ezra Jack. 1971. *Over in the Meadow.* New York: Scholastic Press.

———— . 1977. *Whistle for Willie.* New York: Penguin Books (Puffin Books).

———— . 1983. *Peter's Chair.* New York: Harper & Row.

———— . 1987. *The Snowy Day.* New York: Scholastic.

Kraus, Robert. 1971. *Leo the Late Bloomer.* New York: Windmill Books.

———— . 1972. *Whose Mouse Are You?* New York: Macmillan Publishing Co. (Aladdin Books).

———— . 1977. *Ladybug, Ladybug.* New York: Dutton.

Krauss, Ruth. 1945. *The Carrot Seed.* New York: Harper & Row.

Langstaff, John. 1974. *Oh, A-Hunting We Will Go.* New York: Macmillan Publishing (Atheneum Books).

Martin, Bill. 1970a. *Brown Bear, Brown Bear.* New York: Holt, Rinehart and Winston.

———— . 1970b. *Fire! Fire! Said Mrs. Mcguire.* New York: Holt, Rinehart and Winston.

———— . 1970c. *A Ghost Story.* New York: Holt, Rinehart and Winston.

———— . 1970d. *The Haunted House.* New York: Holt, Rinehart and Winston.

———— . 1970e. *Monday, Monday, I Like Monday.* New York: Holt, Rinehart and Winston.

———— . 1970f. *Up and Down the Escalators.* New York: Holt, Rinehart and Winston.

———— . 1970g. *When It Rains, It Rains.* New York: Holt, Rinehart and Winston.

———— . 1989. *Chicka Chicka Boom Boom.* New York: Scholastic.

Mayer, Mercer. 1967. *A Boy, a Dog and a Frog.* New York: Dial.

———— . 1976. *There's a Nightmare in My Closet.* New York: Dial.

McPhail, David. 1972. *The Bear's Toothache.* Boston: Little, Brown.

McQueen, Lucinda. 1985. *The Little Red Hen.* New York: Scholastic.

Melser, June. 1987. *Lazy Mary.* San Diego: The Wright Group.

Melser, June and Joy Cowley. 1980. *In a Dark, Dark Wood.* Auckland, New Zealand: Shortland Publications (The Wright Group).

———— . 1987a. *The Big Toe.* San Diego: The Wright Group.

———— . 1987b. *One Cold Wet Night.* San Diego: The Wright Group.

———— . 1987c. *Three Little Ducks.* San Diego: The Wright Group.

———— . 1987d. *Yes Ma'am.* San Diego: The Wright Group.

Most, Bernard. 1984. *If the Dinosaurs Came Back.* New York: Harcourt Brace Jovanovich.

Nodset, Joan. 1963. *Who Took the Farmer's Hat?* New York: Scholastic Press.

Parks, Brenda. 1986. *Who's in the Shed?* Crystal Lake, IL: Rigby Education.

Peek, Merle. 1985. *Mary Wore Her Red Dress and Henry Wore His Green Sneakers.* New York: Clarion.

Sendak, Maurice. 1962. *Alligators All Around.* New York: Harper & Row.

———. 1965. *Where the Wild Things Are.* New York: Harper and Brothers.

———. 1986. *Chicken Soup With Rice.* New York: Scholastic.

Slobodkina, Esphyr. 1984. *Caps for Sale.* New York: Scholastic.

Titherington, Jeanette. 1986. *Pumpkin, Pumpkin.* New York: Greenwillow Books.

Tolstoy, Alexei. 1968. *The Great Big Enormous Turnip.* New York: Franklin Watts.

Ward, Leila. 1978. *I Am Eyes-Ni Macho.* New York: Scholastic.

Wells, Rosemary. 1973. *Noisy Nora.* New York: Dial.

———. 1980. *Benjamin and Tulip.* New York: Dial.

Wildsmith, Brian. 1978. *What the Moon Saw.* Toronto: Oxford University Press.

———. 1986. *What A Tale.* New York: Oxford University Press.

———. 1985. *Toot, Toot.* Toronto: Oxford University Press.

Williams, Rebel. 1990. *The Nine Days of Camping.* San Diego: The Wright Group.

Wood, Audrey. 1980. *Twenty-four Robbers.* Singapore: Child's Play (International) Ltd.

———. 1984. *The Napping House.* San Diego: Harcourt Brace Jovanovich.

Wood, Leslie. 1986. *Bump, Bump, Bump.* Toronto: Oxford University Press.

Zemach, Margot. 1965. *The Teeny Tiny Woman.* New York: Scholastic.

## PATTERNED LANGUAGE BOOK SERIES

McCracken, Robert and Marlene. 1989. *Tiger Cub Readers.* Winnipeg: Peguis Press.

The Sunshine Reading Series. 1986. Bothell, WA: The Wright Group.

Williams, Rebel. 1990. *Twig Books.* Bothell, WA: The Wright Group.

Wonder World Books. 1993. Bothell, WA: The Wright Group.

## BOOKS FOR MORE FLUENT READERS

Aardema, Verna. 1978. *Why Mosquitoes Buzz in People's Ears.* New York: Dial.

———. 1981. *Bringing the Rain to Kapiti Plain.* New York: Dial.

Allard, Harry. 1978-1986. *Miss Nelson* books. New York: Scholactic.

Barrett, Judi. 1978. *Cloudy With a Chance of Meatballs.* New York: Scholastic.

Berenstain, Stan and Jan Berenstain. 1970. *Old Hat/New Hat.* New York: Random House.

———. 1974. *He Bear/She Bear.* New York: Random House.

———. 1978a. *Bears In the Night.* New York: Random House.

———. 1978b. *The Berenstain Bears and The Spooky Old Tree!* New York: Random House.

Brett, Jan. 1983. *The Twelve Days of Christmas. New York: Dodd, Mead & Co.*

———. 1989. *The Mitten.* New York: Scholastic Inc.

Bridwell, Norman. 1984-1986. *Clifford* Books. New York: Scholastic.

Brown, Marc. 1981a. *Arthur's Eyes.* New York: Avon Books (Camelot Books).

———. 1981b. *Arthur's Nose.* New York: Avon Books (Camelot Books).

———. 1984. *Arthur Goes to Camp.* Boston: Little Brown.

Brown, Marcia. 1975. *Stone Soup.* New York: Charles Scribner and Sons.

Bryan, Ashley. 1989. *Turtle Knows Your Name.* New York: Macmillan. (Atheneum Books).

Cherry, Lynne. 1990. *The Great Kapok Tree.* San Diego: Harcourt Brace Jovanovich.

Cohen, Miriam. 1971. *Will I Have a Friend?* New York: Macmillan.

———— . 1976. *Best Friends.* New York: Macmillan.

———— . 1977. *When Will I Read?* New York: Greenwillow Books.

———— . 1985. *Starring First Grade.* New York: Greenwillow Books.

Cole, Babette. 1987. *Princess Smartypants.* New York: G.P. Putnam.

Crofts, Trudy and Ken McKeon. 1976. *The Hunter and the Quail: Tales of the Buddha.* Emeryville, CA: Dharma Publishing.

de Paola, Tomie. 1975. *Strega Nona.* Englewood Cliffs, NJ: Prentice-Hall.

Demi. 1980. *Liang and the Magic Paintbrush.* New York: Henry Holt.

Eastman, P. D. 1960. *Are You My Mother?* New York: Beginner Books.

———— . 1961. *Go Dog Go!* New York: Random House.

Feelings, Muriel. 1974. *Jambo Means Hello.* New York: Dial.

Galdone, Paul. 1975. *The Gingerbread Boy.* New York: Clarion Books.

———— . 1978. *Cinderella.* New York: McGraw-Hill.

———— . 1985. *Rumpelstiltskin.* New York: Clarion Books.

Gantos, Jack. 1976. *Rotten Ralph.* Boston: Houghton Mifflin.

Goble, Paul. 1978. *The Girl Who Loved Wild Horses.* New York: Bradbury Press.

———— . 1984. *Buffalo Woman.* New York: Bradbury Press.

Graham, Margaret Bloy. 1976. *Harry the Dirty Dog.* New York: Harper & Row.

Greenfield, Eloise. 1984. *Me and Neesie.* New York: Harper & Row.

Gross, Ruth Belov. 1988. *Hansel and Gretel.* New York: Scholastic.

Hiawyn, Oram. 1984. *In the Attic.* New York: Henry Holt.

Hoban, Lillian. 1982. *Arthur's Honey Bear.* New York: Harper & Row.

———— . 1984. *Arthur's Prize Reader.* New York: Harper & Row.

Hoban, Russell and Lillian Hoban. 1976–1986. *Frances* books. New York: Harper & Row.

Hoban, Russell. 1964. *Bread and Jam for Frances.* New York: Harper & Row.

Hoff, Syd. 1976. *Danny and the Dinosaur.* New York: Harper & Row.

Hogrogian, Nonny. 1971. *One Fine Day.* New York: Macmillan.

Isadora, Rachel. 1991. *At the Crossroads.* New York: Scholastic.

Jarrell, Randall. 1980. *The Fisherman and His Wife.* New York: Farrar, Straus & Giroux.

Jeffers, Susan. 1980. *Hansel and Gretel.* New York: Dial.

Jeschke, Susan. 1985. *Perfect the Pig.* New York: Holt, Rinehart and Winston.

Lobel, Arnold. 1970-1985. *Frog and Toad* books. New York: Scholastic.

———— . 1978. *Mouse Tales.* New York: Harper & Row.

———— . 1986a. *Ming Lo Moves the Mountain.* New York: Scholastic.

———— . 1986b. *Mouse Soup.* New York: Scholastic.

———— . 1987. *Owl at Home.* New York: Harper & Row.

Louie, Ai-Lang. 1982. *Yeh Shen: A Cinderella Story from China.* New York: Philomel Books.

Marshall, James. 1982. *George and Martha* books. Boston: Houghton Mifflin (Sandpiper Books).

———— . 1986a. *The Three Little Pigs.* New York: Dial.

———— . 1986b. *Three Up a Tree.* New York: Dial Books for Young Readers.

———— . 1988. *Goldilocks and the Three Bears.* New York: Dial.

McDermott, Gerald. 1972. *Anansi the Spider: A Tale from the Ashanti.* New York: Holt, Rinehart and Winston.

———— . 1974. *Arrow to the Sun: A Pueblo Indian Tale.* New York: Viking Press.

McGovern, Ann. 1967. *Too Much Noise.* Boston: Houghton Mifflin.

McKissack, Patricia. 1988. *Mirandy and Brother Wind.* New York: Knopf.

———— . 1989. *Nettie Jo's Friends.* New York: Knopf.

McPhail, David. 1980. *Pig Pig Grows Up.* New York: Dutton.

Miles, Miska. 1971. *Annie and the Old One.* New York: Little Brown.

Minarik, Elsie Holmelund. 1979. *Little Bear* books. New York: Harper & Row.

Mosel, Arlene. 1984a. *The Funny Little Woman.* New York: E.P. Dutton.

————. 1984b. *Tikki Tikki Tembo.* New York: Scholastic.

Numeroff, Laura Joffe. 1985. *If You Give a Mouse a Cookie.* New York: Harper & Row.

————. 1992. *If You Give a Moose a Muffin.* New York: Harper & Row.

Polacco, Patricia. 1988. *Rechenka's Eggs.* New York: Philomel Books.

————. 1992. *Chicken Sunday.* New York: Philomel Books.

————. 1993. *The Bee Tree.* New York: Philomel Books.

Rayner, Mary. 1979. *Mr. and Mrs. Pig's Evening Out.* New York: Macmillan (Aladdin Books).

Rey, H.A. and Margaret Rey. 1969-1985. *Curious George* books. Boston: Houghton Mifflin, and New York: Scholastic.

Ringgold, Faith. 1991. *Tar Beach.* New York: Scholastic.

Schwartz, Alvin. 1984. *The Dark, Dark Room and Other Scary Stories.* New York: Harper & Row.

Scieszka, Jon. 1989. *The True Story of The Three Little Pigs by A. Wolf.* New York: Viking.

Seuss, Dr. 1957. *The Cat in the Hat.* New York: Beginner Books.

————. 1960a. *Green Eggs and Ham.* New York: Random House.

————. 1960b. *One Fish Two Fish Red Fish Blue Fish.* New York: Beginner Books.

————. 1963. *Hop on Pop.* New York: Beginner Books.

————. 1965. *Fox in Socks.* New York: Beginner Books.

————. 1978. *I Can Read with My Eyes Shut!* New York: Beginner Books.

Slepian, Jan and Ann Seidler. 1987. *The Cat Who Wore a Pot on Her Head.* New York: Scholastic.

Steig, William. 1969. *Sylvester and the Magic Pebble.* New York: Simon and Schuster.

————. 1982. *Doctor De Soto.* New York: Farrar, Straus & Giroux.

Steptoe, John. 1987. *Mufaro's Beautiful Daughters.* New York: Lothrop, Lee & Shepard.

Sueling, Barbara. 1976. *The Teeny Tiny Woman.* New York: Viking.

Surat, Michele Maria. 1983. *Angel Child, Dragon Child.* Milwaukee, WI: Raintree.

Tresselt, Alvin. 1964. *The Mitten.* New York: Lothrop, Lee & Shepard.

Viorst, Judith. 1976. *Alexander and the Terrible, Horrible, No Good, Very Bad Day.* New York: Macmillan Publishing Company (Aladdin Books).

————. 1979. *Rosie and Michael.* New York: Macmillan (Aladdin Books).

————. 1980. *Alexander Who Used to Be Rich Last Sunday.* Macmillan (Atheneum Books).

Vipont, Elfrida and Raymond Briggs. 1986. *The Elephant and the Bad Baby.* New York: Coward-McCann.

Waber, Bernard. 1967. *An Anteater Named Arthur.* Boston: Houghton Mifflin.

————. 1984. *Ira Sleeps Over.* Boston: Houghton Mifflin (Sandpiper Books).

Winter, Jeanette. 1988. *Follow the Drinking Gourd.* New York: The Trumpet Club.

Wiseman, Bernard. 1978. *Morris Has a Cold.* New York: Scholastic.

————. 1983. *Morris Goes to School.* New York: Harper & Row.

————. 1988. *Morris and Boris at the Circus.* New York: Harper & Row.

Yarbrough, Camille. 1979. *Cornrows.* New York: Coward, McCann & Geoghegan.

Young, Ed. 1989. *Lon Po Po: A Red-Riding Hood Story from China.* New York: Scholastic.

Zemach, Margot. 1983. *The Little Red Hen: An Old Story.* New York: Farrar, Straus & Giroux.

Zolotow, Charlotte. 1972. *William's Doll.* New York: Harper & Row.

## POEMS, RHYMES, AND SONGS

Adoff, Arnold. 1973. *Black Is Brown Is Tan.* New York: Harper & Row.

Ahlberg, Janet and Allen Ahlberg. 1979. *Each Peach Pear Plum.* New York: Viking.

Carle, Eric. 1989. *Animals Animals.* New York: Philomel Books.

Cole, Joanna and Stephanie Calmenson. 1991. *The Eentsy, Weentsy Spider: Fingerplays and Action Rhymes.* New York: Mulberry Books.

deRegniers, Beatrice Schenk. 1988. *Sing a Song of Popcorn.* New York: Scholastic.

Fujikawa, Gyo. 1977. *Mother Goose.* New York: Grosset & Dunlap.

Greenfield, Eloise. 1986. *Honey I Love and Other Poems.* New York: Harper & Row.

Griego, Margot C., et al. 1981. *Tortillas Para Mama: and Other Spanish Nursery Rhymes.* New York: Holt, Rinehart and Winston.

Hopkins, Lee B., ed. 1984. *Surprises.* New York: Harper & Row.

Hurd, Thacher. 1985. *Mama Don't Allow.* New York: Harper & Row.

Keats, Ezra Jack. 1985. *Over in the Meadow.* New York: Scholastic.

Langstaff, John. 1974. *Oh, A-Hunting We Will Go.* New York: Atheneum.

————. 1957. *Over in the Meadow.* New York: Harcourt Brace Jovanovich.

Lobel, Arnold. 1985. *Whiskers & Rhymes.* New York: Scholastic.

O'Neill, Mary. 1989. *Hailstones and Halibut Bones.* New York: Doubleday.

Pomerantz, Charlotte. 1993. *Poems in Eleven Languages: If I Had a Paka.* New York: Greenwillow Books.

Prelutsky, Jack. 1976. *Nightmares: Poems to Trouble Your Sleep.* New York: Greenwillow Books.

————. 1980. *Rolling Harvey Down the Hill.* New York: Greenwillow Books.

————. 1983. *The Random House Book of Poetry for Children.* New York: Random House.

————. 1986. *Read-Aloud Rhymes for the Very Young.* New York: Knopf.

————. 1990. *Something Big Has Been Here.* New York: Greenwillow Books.

Raffi. 1987. *Shake My Sillies Out.* New York: Crown.

————. 1988a. *Baby Beluga.* New York: Crown.

————. 1988b. *Wheels on the Bus.* New York: Crown.

Reid, Barbara. 1987. *Sing a Song of Mother Goose.* New York: Scholastic.

Schwartz, Alvin. 1989. *I Saw You in the Bathtub and Other Folk Rhymes.* New York: Harper Collins.

Silverstein, Shel. 1974. *Where the Sidewalk Ends.* New York: Harper & Row.

————. 1981. *A Light in the Attic.* New York: Harper & Row.

Spier, Peter. 1961. *The Fox Went Out on a Chilly Night.* New York: Doubleday.

Watson, Clyde. 1971. *Father Fox's Pennyrhymes.* New York: Scholastic Press.


## NONFICTION BOOKS AND MAGAZINES

### Books:

Adler, David A. 1989a. *A Picture Book of Abraham Lincoln.* New York: The Trumpet Club.

————. 1989b. *A Picture Book of George Washington.* New York: The Trumpet Club.

————. 1989c. *A Picture Book of Martin Luther King, Jr.* New York: Scholastic.

Back, Christine and Jens Olesen. 1982. *Chicken and Egg*. New York: The Trumpet Club.
Back, Christine and Barrie Watts. 1986. *Bean and Plant*. Englewood Cliffs, NJ: Silver Burdett.
Cox, Victor. 1989. *The Living Ocean*. New York: Random House.
Gibbons, Gail. 1984. *Tunnels*. New York: Holiday House.
———. 1987. *Dinosaurs*. New York: Holiday House.
Heller, Ruth. 1981. *Chickens Aren't the Only Ones*. New York: Grosset & Dunlap.
———. 1987. *Animals Born Alive and Well*. New York: Scholastic.
Hoffman, Mary. 1992. *Seal*. (Animals in the Wild). New York: Steck-Vaughn.
———. 1987. *Bear*. (Animals in the Wild). New York: Scholastic.
Hornblow, Leonora and Arthur Hornblow. 1964. *Animals Do the Strangest Things*. New York: Random House.
Hou-tien, Cheng. 1976. *The Chinese New Year*. New York: Holt, Rinehart and Winston.
Lowery, Linda. 1987. *Martin Luther King Day*. New York: Scholastic.
Marzello, Jean. 1993. *Happy Birthday Martin Luther King*. New York: Scholastic.
Parker, Nancy Winslow and Joan Richards Wright. 1990. *Frogs, Toads, Lizards, and Salamanders*. New York: Greenwillow Books.
Seymour, Simon. 1989a. *Deserts*. New York: Morrow.
———. 1989b. *Stars*. New York: Morrow.
———. 1989c. *Storms*. New York: Morrow.

## Series of Books:

*Eyewitness Junior Books*. 1991. New York: Alfred A. Knopf. A series about science-related topics, including wolves, shells, and fish.
*The Fascinating World of . . .* 1991. New York: Barron's Educational Series. A series about living creatures (e.g., ants, bees, and birds)
*A First Discovery Book*. 1989. New York: Scholastic. A series about animals, insects, color, etc.
*I Want to Know About . . . A New True Book*. 1981. Chicago: Children's Press. A set of twenty-six books on various topics of interest to young children, including animals, space, and insects.
*Let's-Read-and-Find-Out Science Book*. New York: Harper & Row. This series presents basic science information on a range of topics, including health, weather, animals, and planets.

## Magazines:

*Ranger Rick*. Washington, DC: National Wildlife Federation.
*World*. Washington, DC: National Geographic Society.
*Your Big Backyard*. Washington, DC: National Wildlife Federation.
*Zoo Books*. San Diego, CA: Wildlife Education, Ltd.

# References

Babbitt, Natalie. 1987. *Tuck Everlasting* (ils.). New York: Bantam.

*Becoming a Nation of Readers: The Report of the Commission on Reading*. 1984. Washington, DC: The National Institute of Education. Available from the National Council of Teachers of English, Urbana, IL.

Chomsky, Carol. 1972. Stages in Language Development and Reading Exposure. *Harvard Educational Review* 42: 1–33.

Clay, Marie. 1982. *Observing Young Readers: Collected Papers*. Portsmouth, NH: Heinemann.

Cook, Barbara and Carole Urzúa. 1993. *The Literacy Club: A Cross-age Tutoring/ Paired Reading Project*. Washington, DC: National Clearinghouse for Bilingual Education.

Crew, Linda. 1989. *Children of the River*. New York: Dell.

Durkin, Dolores. 1966. *Children Who Read Early: Two Longitudinal Studies*. New York: Teachers College Press.

Edelsky, Carole. 1988. Living in the Author's World: Analyzing the Author's Craft. *The California Reader* 21: 12–17.

Eeds, Maryann and Deborah Wells. 1989. Grand Conversations: An Exploration of Meaning Construction in Literature Study Groups. *Research in the Teaching of English* 23: 4–29.

Gibbs, Jeanne. 1994. *Tribes: A New Way of Learning Together*. Santa Rosa, CA: Center Source Publications.

Hansen, Joyce. 1991. *Yellow Bird and Me* (ils.). Boston, MA: Clarion.

Heath, Shirley Brice and Leslie Mangiola. 1991. *Children of Promise: Literate Activity in Linguistically and Culturally Diverse Classrooms*. Washington, DC: National Education Association.

Holdaway, Don. 1979. *The Foundations of Literacy*. Auckland, New Zealand: Ashton Scholastic.

Juel, Connie. 1991. Cross-Age Tutoring Between Student Athletes and At-Risk Children. *The Reading Teacher* 45 (3): 178–186.

Labbo, Linda D. and William H. Teale. 1990. Cross-Age Reading: A Strategy for Helping Poor Readers. *The Reading Teacher* 43 (6): 362–369.

Leland, Christine and Ruth Fitzpatrick. 1994. Cross-Age Interaction Builds Enthusiasm for Reading and Writing. *The Reading Teacher* 47 (4): 292–301.

Morrice, Connie and Maureen Simmons. 1991. Beyond Reading Buddies: A Whole Language Cross-Age Program. *The Reading Teacher* 44 (8): 572–577.

Peterson, Ralph and Maryann Eeds. 1990. *Grand Conversations: Literature Groups in Action*. New York: Scholastic.

Samway, Katharine Davies, Gail Whang, Carl Cade, Melindevic Gamil, Mary Ann Lubandina, and Kansone Phommachanh. 1991. Reading the Skeleton, the Heart, and the Brain of a Book: Students' Perspectives on Literature Study Circles. *The Reading Teacher* 45 (3): 196–205.